D0426717

From the Library of

KEEP A TRUE LENT

Also by Charles Fillmore

ATOM-SMASHING POWER OF MIND

THE CHARLES FILLMORE CONCORDANCE

CHRISTIAN HEALING

DYNAMICS FOR LIVING

JESUS CHRIST HEALS

METAPHYSICAL BIBLE DICTIONARY

MYSTERIES OF GENESIS

MYSTERIES OF JOHN

PROSPERITY

THE REVEALING WORD

TALKS ON TRUTH

TEACH US TO PRAY

THE TWELVE POWERS OF MAN

Keep a True Lent

Charles Fillmore

Unity Classic Library

Unity Village, MO 64065

Keep a True Lent is a member of the Unity Classic Library.

The Unity Classic Library is guided by the belief of Unity cofounder Charles Fillmore that "whatever God has revealed to man in one age He will continue to reveal to him in all ages." The series projects Fillmore's vision of Unity as "a link in the great educational movement inaugurated by Jesus Christ" to help and teach humankind to use and prove eternal Truth.

To receive a catalog of all Unity publications (books, cassettes, compact discs, and magazines) or to place an order, call the Customer Service Department: (816) 969-2069 or 1-800-669-0282. For information, address Unity Books, Publishers, Unity School of Christianity, 1901 NW Blue Parkway, Unity Village, MO 64065-0001.

Sixteenth printing 1999

Cover design by Jill L. Ziegler

Library of Congress Catalog Card Number: 89-51042
ISBN 0-87159-073-5
Canada BN 13252 9033 RT

Unity Books feels a sacred trust to be a healing presence in the world. By printing with biodegradable soybean ink on recycled paper, we believe we are doing our part to be wise stewards of our Earth's resources.

"Lent is a season of spiritual growth, a time for progressive unfoldment. When we can blend and merge our mind with God-Mind, the way is open for the Lord to glorify us and to lift us into a higher, purer, more spiritual state."

Charles Fillmore

FOREWORD

THE CHRISTIAN world is once again observing the Lenten season; the season of prayer and fasting that precedes the joyous festivity of Easter. It is commonly believed that the Lenten period has to do with the events of the forty days preceding the Resurrection. This is an erroneous idea. Lent is a church institution, and there is no authorization for it anywhere in the New Testament. The idea, however, has a sound spiritual basis; Moses, Elijah, and Jesus Himself set a precedent for it. Each observed a forty-day period of prayer and fasting as a preparation for spiritual work. Moses received the Ten Commandments on Mount Sinai at the conclusion of his fast. Elijah talked with God on Mount Horeb at the conclusion of his period of prayer and fasting. Jesus began His great spiritual ministry at the close of His fast in the wilderness.

The ancient Hebrew writers made a practice of using numbers to symbolize ideas. Forty, in their minds, was a "foursquare" number suggesting the idea of a foundation for something to follow; an idea of completeness. So the number forty is frequently used in the Scriptures to indicate a completed preparation for something to follow. When we consider Lent as a well-rounded or "completed" season of retreat from the things of the world for the cleansing of the mind and the recollection of the things of Spirit, it becomes a true season of preparation for the glorious Eastertide; a preparation for the resurrection of the mind from the darkness of its sins, doubts, and false beliefs into the light of understanding.

Lent, then, is a church institution embodying an exalted idea, the idea of cleansing and disciplining both mind and body toward the end of making them more receptive to the Christ ideas. Like many other religious practices it is too often observed in letter but not in spirit.

Too many people make a fad out of Lent. It is fashionable to give up some luxuries, and when those luxuries have to do with food and drink it is profitable physically. There is also psychological value in the mental discipline involved. But such observance has nothing to do with being a Christian; atheists could get the same benefit!

Every follower of Jesus who would keep Lent in the true Christian spirit follows the way of prayer and fasting that He taught His disciples. He revealed that prayer and fasting are the sure way to spiritual power, the way to keep the soul cleansed and purified that it may feel the presence of God. When the disciples were unable to heal the epileptic boy He told them that they lacked faith, that such healings could only be brought about by prayer and fasting.

Jesus revealed that fasting, like prayer, is a matter between man and his Maker. He told His disciples that they were to make no show of their fasting. He said, "Appear not unto men to fast, but unto thy Father which is in secret: and thy Father, which seeth in secret, shall reward thee openly." He gave the same instruction concerning prayer. Prayer and fasting, then, are matters of communion with God, not matters of public display. They are transactions in mind. It is of no use to go through the outer form if the feeling of communion with God is not established. In abstinence from worldly things the mind must be filled with thoughts of God, else there is no spiritual value in fasting.

If we would "lose the bands of wickedness" we must learn to fast from all unworthy thought and feast on the good and the true. To observe Lent according to the spirit rather than the letter we must fast from criticism and condemnation and feast in brotherly love; fast from false beliefs in sickness and weakness and feast on the truth of God's omnipresent, perfect life; fast from false beliefs in lack and limitation and feast on the truth of God's bountiful good will. Ideas such as these form an excellent basis for Lenten meditations that help establish permanent spiritual values in heart and mind.

One of the most valuable ways of observing the Lenten season is to fast from (loose and let go) the belief that men or nations can stand in the way of God's good will for man. Now is the time to affirm the power of the Christ Spirit indwelling in all men everywhere and influencing their thoughts, words, and actions to work for the good of the whole. We all want to be of some influence in establishing world peace. To do so we must learn to obey Paul's exhortation "Let us therefore follow after the things which make for peace." Each one of us must be concerned with improving his own life. We must learn to deny our selfish impulses and be obedient to impulses of brotherly love. When we withdraw our attention, interest, and support from the false and the unworthy, this is true fasting. When we give that same attention, interest, and support to the enduring good, we are feasting on the things of the Spirit, and this is true prayer. When we have truly fasted in the Christ way we have increased our ability to respond to God's good will.

—Georgiana Tree West

PUBLISHER'S NOTE—Some Unity students will note that they have previously read some of the material in *"Keep A True Lent."* Some of the material in this book originally appeared in *Unity* magazine and portions of it may be found in other books by Charles Fillmore. The material was assembled in this manner in order that this book would offer the reader a well-rounded course of study during Lent.

CONTENTS

The Lenten Lessons

The Way to Perfection

Chapter 1

"I AM GOD ALMIGHTY; walk before me, and be thou perfect."

In prayer we need to be deeply conscious that God is the almighty One, the supreme Creator the ruler of the universe, that He is infinite and eternal; we need to know that God is the underlying, unchangeable Truth, "with whom can be no variation, neither shadow that is cast by turning."

God as principle is the absolute good expressed in all creation. When we know God and "worship him in spirit and truth" we recognize Him as this great goodness, which is omnipresent, omniscient, omnipotent, ready and willing to guide, to bless, and to uplift.

To walk with almighty God is to walk with Truth and to affirm the power of Spirit within mind and body as the dominating mind force; it is to walk in the light and thus to apply in our daily living the wisdom that is from above, acknowledging the Father as the source of all our knowing, as the mainspring of all our actions.

This leads us to the truth that our knowing God brings peace, the serene abiding that never wearies, never questions, never strains for results. He created and controls the whole universe. In God "we live, and move, and have our being."

Mind is the common meeting ground between God and man, and it is only through the most highly accelerated mind action, as in prayer, that we can consciously make union with God, the one and only Creator.

Prayer is the language of spirituality and improves the quality of man's being. Prayer makes man master in the realm of creative ideas. The inner silence of prayer is a great source of spiritual power. There is no exception to this rule in all the evidence of life. "Be still, and know that I am God."

The living Word of God, the creative idea in Divine Mind, may be expressed by man when he has fulfilled the law of expression. To keep the Word is to revolve it in mind, to go over it in all its aspects, to believe in it as Truth, to treasure it as a saving balm in time of need, and above all, to obey the law it sets forth.

The Christ is God's divine idea of man, the embodiment of all divine ideas existing in the mind of Being. The Christ is the "Messiah," the "anointed one." The Christ is the living principle working in man. "Thou art the Christ, the Son of the living God."

"Know ye not that ye are a temple of God, and *that* the Spirit of God dwelleth in you?" Under the direction of the Christ a new body is constructed by the thinking faculty in man. The materials entering into this superior structure are spiritual substances, and the new creation is the body of Spirit. It breathes an atmosphere and is thrilled with a life energy more real than that of the manifest man. When we come into the realization of our true Christ body we feel the stirring within us of the indwelling Spirit. We know what Paul meant when he said, "There is a natural body, and there is also a spiritual *body.*" The true temple in the "body" of Christ is a state of consciousness. In the inmost center of every man the indwelling Christ resides.

Would you meet your God in this sacred place? Then quietly enter this holy of holies in the name and through the power of Jesus Christ. Here reality reigns supreme. Neither doubt nor fear can enter. You will be conscious only of the great omnipresence of God, where the light, joy, peace, and satisfaction of His Spirit abide, where Truth reigns supreme.

In this inner realm you will find the spiritual ethers heavily charged with ideas that turn to spiritual substance. As your consciousness (awareness) expands, you touch the everlasting truths and you find that every blessing is abundantly added. What seems new is but the unveiling of that which has been forever.

It is of this high realization of oneness with Spirit that Paul wrote in II Cor. 12:4, when the man was "caught up into Paradise, and heard unspeakable words, which it is not lawful for man to utter."

In this realm, attention is given to concentrating

the mind on Truth; the I AM, or inner entity is focalized on God's word until the inner meaning is realized and man is aware of a definite spiritual uplift.

Persistent meditation on the Truth contained in the Word of God opens the mind to a greater inflow of Spirit. Then all words become quickening life and nourishing substance in both mind and body. "Let the word of Christ dwell in you richly."

Your thinking Truth zealously and affirming it audibly will dissolve error in consciousness and at the same time reveal greater spiritual illumination. In this consciousness appropriate words of Truth. "Eat them," so to speak. Partake of that with which you form the spiritual substance and which will manifest itself in the Christ, or perfect body. Let "Christ be formed in you." Know that the Holy Spirit is filling your being with its illuminating, resurrecting power and that the all-knowing One shines in you as it did in Jesus and that you manifest greater and greater spiritual understanding.

When man praises the Spirit of wisdom within he expands and deepens and enriches his consciousness. As the Christ radiance lights man's mind, he sees with the inner eye and he finds that Truth is a never-failing light that makes straight his way.

In this high state of consciousness he knows that the divine perfection that exists in the universal God-Mind is brought into direct contact with its image and likeness, the Christ Spirit that was implanted in him by the Creator from the beginning.

The resurrection of Jesus takes place in us each time we rise to the realization of the perpetual indwelling life that connects us with the Father. The graveclothes of mortal sense, which are thoughts of limitation and inevitable obedience to material laws, are left in the tomb of matter.

True resurrection within us lifts up all the faculties of mind until they conform to the absolute ideas of Divine Mind. This mental renewal makes a complete transformation of the body, so that every function works in divine order and every cell becomes incorruptible and immortal.

For the perpetuation or the renewal of youth in mind and body it is well to affirm often:

"Bless Jehovah, O my soul;
And all that is within me, *bless* his holy name.
Bless Jehovah, O my soul,
And forget not all his benefits:
Who forgiveth all thine iniquities;
Who healeth all thy diseases:
Who redeemeth thy life from destruction;
Who crowneth thee with lovingkindness and tender mercies;
Who satisfieth thy desire with good things,
So that thy youth is renewed like the eagle."

The Holy Trinity

the Father, the Son, and the Holy Spirit

Chapter 2

THE HOLY TRINITY is known as the Father, the Son, and the Holy Spirit. Metaphysically, we understand the Trinity to refer to mind, idea, and expression, or thinker, thought, and action.

God is first in the Trinity. God is mind and is everywhere present. God is principle, law, Being, Spirit, All-Good, omnipotent, omniscient, omnipresent, unchangeable, Creator, Father, cause, and source of all that is. God as Spirit is forever accessible.

God as principle is the unchangeable life, love, substance, and intelligence of Being. A parallel may be found in the principle of mathematics or music. Principle does not occupy space, nor has it any limitations of time or matter, but eternally exists as the one underlying cause from which come forth all true ideas.

In universal God-Mind is a substance that includes the seed of all visible substance. It is the only real substance, because it is unchangeable, while visible substance is in constant transition. God as substance does not mean matter, because matter is formed; God is formless. The substance that God is lies back of all matter and all form. It is that which is the basis of all form, yet enters not into any form as finality. It cannot be seen, tasted, or touched, yet it is the one and only "substantial" substance.

Second in the Trinity is God's idea of man. It is called Jehovah in the Old Testament and Christ in the New Testament. The second in the Trinity is also called the Word, the Son, the Logos, the anointed One, and the I AM.

The Word of God is the revelation to man of the powers and possibilities of his own being. The searchlight of His Word discloses the presence of secret springs and living streams of energy and life. Man's consciousness is lifted up by the wisdom of the Word, and he finds himself master of the powers and privileges of infinity. He says with Jesus, "All authority hath been given unto me in heaven and on earth."

To produce works, there must be a working power. This is exactly what the Word is—the working power of God.

Every known process has a regular sequence from inception to conclusion, and each step in the sequence is taken according to recognized principles. The Word of God conveys to the world the concepts of the Most High.

Persistent meditation on the Truth contained in the Word of God opens the mind to Spirit. Then all words become quickening life and nourishing substance in both mind and body. "Let the word of Christ dwell in you richly."

In the silence go before the altar and lay your problems before the Lord. The altar is that place in consciousness where you are willing to let go of the lesser for the greater, to let go of personality and enter into individuality of the Christ.

While in this closet of prayer, fix your mind powerfully on the consummation of a certain idea until the idea nucleates a certain amount of thought substance. This is followed by a spiritual quickening, or the outpouring of the Holy Spirit, third in the Trinity.

The function of the Holy Spirit implies distinct personal subsistence: He speaks, searches, selects, reveals, reproves, testifies, leads, comforts, distributes to every man, "searcheth all things, yea, the deep things of God."

In concentration the Holy Spirit works through the divine substance to bring forth the fruits of Divine Mind. The Holy Spirit is the teacher. The teacher and the student use the same principles; but the teacher arouses and inspires the student to greater achievement. The Holy Spirit today is urging us to greater spiritual effort.

Another word for the Holy Spirit is "the Comforter," Jesus said: "Nevertheless I tell you the truth: It is expedient for you that I go away; for if I go not away, the Comforter will not come unto you; but if I go, I will send him unto you. And he, when he is come, will convict the world in respect of sin, and of righteousness, and of judgment."

The mission of Jesus was to open the way for the Holy Spirit to enter into the minds of men. "But when the Comforter is come, whom I will send unto you from the Father, *even* the Spirit of truth, which proceedeth from the Father, he shall bear witness of me."

We may understand the relation and office of the Father, the Son, and the Holy Spirit by analyzing our own mind and its apparent subdivisions during thought action, because each person is a perfect image and likeness of this great universal first cause —God, the Father.

Your word is the power through which you make your belief manifest. Simple belief in or assent to the truth of a proposition never gives understanding to anyone. There must be mental action; changes in the mind are necessary before the new state of consciousness takes up its abode in you.

Therefore, in answer to that frequently asked question, "Who is the Holy Spirit, and what relation does it bear to God and to Christ?" the apostles knew the Holy Spirit as the third person of the Trinity. The Father is always the first, the Son or Word second, and the Holy Spirit third. The terms *Father* and *Son* express an eternal, reciprocal relation. The Holy Spirit is the infinite "breath" of God, as the Son of His infinite "Word."

God-Mind is located and appears wherever it is recognized by the mind of man. It thus follows that whoever gives his attention to Spirit and seals his identification with it by his word (the Son) starts a flow of Spirit life and all the attributes of Spirit in and through his consciousness. To the extent that he practices identifying himself with the one and only source of existence, he becomes Spirit in expression, until finally the union attains a perfection in which he can say with Jesus, "I and the Father are one."

In making your demonstrations, work for the conviction in your own heart that you are a son of God; next, declare it in word and carry it out in the acts of your daily life. After declaring it, if you fail in demonstrating yourself to be a son of God, determine why. "Ask, and it shall be given you . . . knock, and it shall be opened unto you." Perhaps you have neglected some of your spiritual powers, or you may be dissipating your energies on the sense plane.

Be that as it may, when you ask in the silence of Spirit to be shown why you do not demonstrate the powers that Jesus of Nazareth demonstrated, the Holy Spirit will in some way reveal to you your lack. How that revealment will come about, no one can tell you. But if you are patient and trustful, you will be guided and directed so that all the links in the chain of your being will be brought together and harmoniously joined, and the Son of God will be revealed in you.

The House Not Made with Hands

Chapter 3

WE, AS METAPHYSICIANS, take special care that we are logical in our reasoning. We hold that all Truth has its origin in Divine Mind. Whatever we can conceive as being true must manifest itself in creation, and if the creation seems to fall short of the divine perfection in any way, it is a fault on our part—either we are not seeing the whole of it, or we are lacking in understanding. And if we hold to our logic that the good can create nothing but good, it will bring us to the right conclusion. Holding to this logic, we find that there are two steps in creation—mind ideates that which it later brings forth in the outer, just as a man works out in his mind his invention before he makes the model. God is the all-potential mind. God creates first in thought, and His idea of creation is perfect, and that idea exists as a perfect model upon which all manifestation rests. The body of man must rest upon a divine body idea in Divine Mind, and it logically follows that the inner life substance and intelligence of all flesh is perfect.

But you say, "I do not have a perfect body; my body is not perfect, I can see that it is material." It may be that you do not understand; that you fail to discern the "Lord's body," which failure, Paul said, is the cause of weakness and sickness and death.

We have a perfect body in mind, and this perfect mind-body expresses itself through our I AM, or the Christ in us; it brings itself into manifestation just as fast as we let it, just as fast as we perceive God in the flesh.

The real source of life is within you. Go within and close the door of materiality. Talk to God about your life problem; begin to release your hidden energies. Make it a daily process and talk little about what you are doing. The incorporation of divine life in the millions of cells composing your body was accomplished in conjunction with Spirit, and the release should be under the same law. If you want to see the real expression of Divine Mind in your body, all you have to do is mentally to image it. Put your I AM identity into it and affirm that the perfect body as idealized in God-Mind is now made manifest in your hands, in your feet, in your heart, and in every part of your organism.

Is this good logic? Will it work? Of course, it will. This is the real secret of metaphysical healing. In the beginning the Word was God, but the Word became flesh and dwelt among men, and they saw Jesus' body, His glory and His perfection. Jesus Christ was the Word of God made manifest. Jesus saved His body from dissolution and raised it up to the heavenly estate, which is substance so pure that no disintegrating force can be found in it. This gives an importance to the body beyond the usual estimate. People think that soul salvation is the object of the Christian life, but Jesus and Paul laid great stress on the ability of man to "lay it down, and . . . take it again," even this "temple of the living God."

Can we save our body from death? Yes—by seeing it as the very temple of God; and this means more than looking at it as if we were looking through a telescope. We must see our body with our mind. We must see it with something more than the intellectual mind. We must see it with Jehovah, the Christ within us.

When the perfect man is conceived in pure reason, the reason of Spirit, and man sees himself as he is in God-Mind, the Lord's body begins at once to appear. We can all see our body with the "single" eye that Jesus spoke of, and through faith in the reality of the invisible body regenerate the flesh. The body is wonderfully obedient to the I AM. It hastens to do its bidding and is renewed and transformed by thought. But so many of us see our body as it appears to mortal sense, unaware that the real continues, while the seeming passes away. We know that we are healed by right thinking, that we can and do raise sick bodies and restore them to health. Where is the limit to healing? There is no limit. Why can we not go right on and perfect the body idea as conceived in Divine Mind? This is where pure reason and logic sustain us. It makes no difference how many people die, or are going to die; the logic is good if it proves the healing of a single illness. It is indeed uplifting to know that there is a divine power behind this universe, that there is a true God; that life has more meaning than the mere piling up of material things; that we can become the real man, and all the pure ideals can be fulfilled here and now.

The real body of God is a living body. Above all, it is a beautiful body, a temple. And God Himself is in that temple, and it is not necessary to have any light but His light, the light of life and health. It is wonderful how quickly our body responds to a thought of life and health, how we can feel a flow of health instantly if we hold the right thought. Just closing our mind to outer things and holding the thought that we are the perfect manifestations of Divine Mind will often heal our body of its illnesses. Disease is not natural. We must let it go, relax, and let Spirit carry on its perfect work in us; and all at once evil or sick conditions disappear, and we are whole. Those who have had divine healings tell us that their best work was done by simply letting go and realizing that there is but one universal Mind and that this Mind makes a perfect body for every man.

We see this proved again and again in the healing power of nature. All doctors admit that the body is restored to health naturally, that neither they nor drugs do the actual healing. What causes the body to be restored? The divine idea of perfection. Our body really is the temple of the living God. The so-called material body has within it and about it the divine perfection. We should not make any separation. We should hold that our body is spiritual and hold nothing else. We must carry out that living true Word which every one of us knows to be the offspring of Divine Mind. "And the Word became flesh, and dwelt among us."

Christ in You

Chapter 4

VOLTAIRE IS CREDITED with saying that if there were no God, men would invent one. The human characteristics of the gods of all religions betray their man-made origin. Not discerning the real character of God, man has thought of Him as acting as man would if he were God. The result is a God who is angry every day, regrets that He made man, drowns the whole human family, and condemns the wicked to the eternal fire of hell if they fail to ask His forgiveness. This God of many of the religions of the day is of such frightful mien that we find it difficult to accept Him as the loving Father that Jesus taught Him to be.

Robert Ingersoll paraphrased "An honest man is the noblest work of God" to "An honest God is the noblest work of man." He was not so far wrong. All inventions are first pictured in the mind of the inventor. So we form a mental picture of everything we conceive, and our conception of God is no exception. We do not see persons and things as we think we see them. What we see is our own conception of them.

We are forced by intuition, logic, and manifest evidence to the conclusion that the Creator of the universe in which we live was and is wise and good. This being true, we cannot accept descriptions of

Him or His acts that contradict that primal conclusion. When we read that "God is angry *with the wicked* every day" we question the understanding of the writer, although the evidence would tend to prove the assumption.

Those who transgress divine law suffer in various ways, and it might well seem that an angry Being is the executioner. However, we know that even those who frame our civil laws are not angry with the persons who break them. Those who conceive of God as a person will invest Him with personal traits, some of which are ridiculous.

We can all understand that a creation which involves complex relations must be governed by laws and orderly acts. Those who get the right conception of the creative source and adjust their minds to its wisdom, purity, power, love, and completeness as the ideal source of perfect man are rewarded by a serene peace and confidence in the final supremacy of justice and righteousness. God is good, and He is the only real power in the universe; consequently, perfection must eventually establish itself in the minds of the law-abiding people and through them in the whole world.

God-Mind presents its perfect ideals to all minds, especially to those that are open to the light of the Christ, by whom the bonds of error thought are broken. Those who have been trained to think of God as a person, as the parent of a family of billions can continue to think of Him as such by adding the attributes of unlimited principle. But they should not make their God a man with the limitations of the human. The natural man thinks that the world in which he lives is the real world and that the thoughts he thinks are the real thoughts. Those who expect the second coming of Jesus look forward to His appearance in a body of flesh similar to the body that was crucified, if not the same.

But Jesus at the Ascension broke His physical organism into its primal electrons or ions of substance and life, which He sowed as a body seed for all those who follow Him in the regeneration. Thousands have appropriated these seeds of the new Christ body in the past nineteen hundred years and are now in the process of unfolding a redeemed organism. No one has fully developed the Christ body as it will appear when mortal life has been replaced by immortality. Many are experiencing strange sensations that they or their medical advisers do not understand. These are the transforming elements of the new life that they have incorporated into their consciousness in this or some other incarnation.

The redemptive work that Jesus began will require a long period of time to be fulfilled. He told His apostles that many things would happen before the consummation of what He called the "end of the age." This phrase appears in the American Standard Version of the New Testament as the "end of the world," but is corrected in the margin. This erroneous translation, "the end of the world," has caused wave after wave of fear to sweep over the earth for hundreds of years, and many ministers are still using it as a club to scare people into conversion.

Jesus never taught that God would destroy the earth, but He did teach that race evolution was being carried forward in great periods or ages, one of which was ending in His time. Jesus said that no one knew the duration of this age except the Father. Paul doubtless had this in mind when he wrote to the Colossians concerning "the mystery which hath been hid for ages and generations . . . which is Christ in you, the hope of glory." Through Christ we are unified with God and become joint heirs with Jesus to all the treasures of the kingdom of heaven.

Every follower of Jesus should strive for a better and fuller understanding of the unity He made with the Father, whereby He opened the way for us to make the same unity and help others to do likewise. People are no longer herded into heaven by persons preaching the fear of hell, but many persons are sinking deeper and deeper into the delusions of sense. The old serpent is deceiving them with the promise that they get pleasure out of sensations of the flesh. We must preach and teach and demonstrate that there is health and happiness in the spiritual life of Christ. The blood of Jesus does save. We have a striking illustration of the efficacy of human blood in the restoration of life to our wounded soldiers. The blood of the human family has become corrupt, and the race body is no longer vitalized sufficiently. It has reached a point where an infusion of purified blood is imperative.

Jesus raised the blood of His body to spiritual potency. This purified blood was sown as seed in our race thought and can be appropriated by anyone who raises his thoughts to those of Jesus. This is accomplished through faith in Jesus to save one from sin, to inspire one with His Spirit, or through asking Jesus to come to the aid of the sin-sick mind or suffering body. A single atom of the purified blood of Jesus can begin a vitalizing and purifying work in mind and body that will continue until the Christ man appears. How long it will take to transform the mortal into the immortal no man can tell. We do know, however, that once the mind receives the Christ quickening it will continue to grow in grace, incarnation after incarnation, until the rejuvenating life has overcome death and reincarnation is no longer necessary.

The multitudes who still labor under the logic of the personal-God consciousness continue to ask why God does not plainly reveal Himself and destroy the Adversary, who is leading so many astray.

Those who have for even a short time given their thoughts to the Christ Spirit can testify that it has developed in them a new outlook on life. Where before they were doubtful and uncertain, they now have the assurance of the presence of a power that is helping them to better living in every way. Christ has become a real Comforter, working with them, rather than a historical God-man in heaven. Health and prosperity have replaced the former fear of sickness and financial worry.

How great is the need for a metaphysical understanding of God and His relation to man! Jesus taught plainly that "God is Spirit." God is not a sleight-of-hand performer who makes full-grown animals instantly. God gives Himself to man, and man has the power to make himself what he will. Freedom of will is man's inheritance, and he can use that freedom to build or destroy as he determines. Jesus claimed that all authority was given to Him "in heaven and on earth." What Jesus had, we all have potentially. He developed His powers and was the great example for all of us. We can attain the same unity with the Father-Mind that He attained; and He promised us that He will help us to reach this unity with the Father. If suffering humanity could appreciate the importance of this stupendous invitation and accept it, the world and its people would soon be transformed.

The Throne of Love

Chapter 5

DIVINE LOVE is the force that dissolves all the opposers of true thought and thus smooths out every obstacle that presents itself. When love ascends the throne and takes complete possession of our life its rule is just and righteous. Even destructive faculties, such as resistance, opposition, obstinacy, anger, jealousy, are harmonized through love. Perfect love casts out all fear. When love harmonizes the consciousness we find that our outer affairs are put in order and that where once there seemed to be opposition and fear co-operation and trust prevail.

We demonstrate nonresistance by denying all intellectual opposition or antagonism. When the substance of divine love is poured out upon all alien thoughts we are not bothered by them any more. This leads to joy, a positive force that has not been bearing fruit because of the obstructions heaped upon it by the failure to fulfill the law of the All-Good. The wonderful kingdom within man is developed through keeping the commandments; that is, commanding, controlling, and directing every thought according to the harmonious law of love to one another.

The dissolving power of spiritual love is the antidote for a dictatorial will, but we must deny all selfish desires out of our love before we use it in softening the imperious will. When the consciousness of love stands in the inner court of our being we cannot help acceding to its demands. Unselfish love is fearless, because of its forgetfulness of self. Will divides its dominion with love when it is approached in the right attitude; that is, with understanding. Understanding of the law is necessary in all permanent unions. When we know Truth we know that we are all one, that there is no separation whatever. They that love without the adulteration of selfishness or the lust of sense come into the very presence of God.

There is a distinction between love of the divine type, exercised by divine man, and love of the human type, exercised by the mortal man. It requires discriminating judgment to distinguish between human and divine love. All love is divine in its origin, but in passing through the prism of man's mind it is apparently broken into many colors. Yet, like the ray of white light, it ever remains pure. It is within man's province to make its manifestation in his life just as pure as its origin. This, too, requires painstaking discrimination and good judgment. We learn by experience that love must be directed by wisdom. If we give up blindly to the impulses suggested by human love, we shall suffer many downfalls.

David represents love passing through some of these experiences. He let his affections go out to many wives; he attached himself through the heart to the many sources of sensation that the love nature opens. When one gives up to all the emotions engendered by love there is a saturnalia of sensation in consciousness.

The first step in all reform is the recognition of the power of the law. Wisdom shows us what the law is and where we have fallen short in our use of it. Then we are shown that there is no anger against us on the part of God. Transgression of the law brings its own punishment. We are not punished for our sins but by them. God is kindness, God is love—loving-kindness is a word of rare compound.

One good definition of love is that it is the feeling that excites desire for the welfare of its object. If all people would recognize love as embodying this ideal—recognize that God loves all men to the degree that He has poured out His life and substance and intelligence equally with us in the universal scheme—they would find in it the solution to every problem of life. Our greatest good comes in the welfare of all. Jesus recognized divine sonship and universal brotherhood. We confess Jesus as the Son of God, and by that confession we acknowledge that all men are sons of God. All of us want to know Truth and the help that comes from it, but when it is presented to us we object to the broad spirit that it proclaims. This is especially the case if our religious training has been narrow and pharisaical.

The Jews were taught that they were the chosen people and that all others were barbarians. Such doctrine is the foundation of the caste system. When a man begins to see himself better than other men, the thought of superiority extends to his environment, and social apartness follows. What those in authority have taught and what the customs and beliefs of the past have been are of more weight than reason and logic. An innovation on old methods of thought is resisted. The whole religious nature is moved; thought runs to meet thought, and a concentration of resistance is set up in the mind.

Many persons wonder why they do not develop divine love more quickly. Here is the reason: They make a wall of separation between the religious and the secular, between the good and the bad. Divine love sees no distinction among persons. It is Principle and it feels its own perfection everywhere. It feels the same in the heart of the sinner as it does in the heart of the saint. When we let the Truth of Being into our heart and pull down all walls of separation we shall feel the flow of infinite love that Jesus felt.

A sense of oneness is a natural product of love, and it is accompanied by a consciousness of security. Through our sense of oneness with the All-Good, the greatest possible sense of security is realized; therefore, all fear is readily and completely cast out. John emphasizes the fact that in order to love God we must necessarily love our fellow men. A love that is adulterated in any degree by hatred for anything or anybody is not pure enough to discern the great love of the Infinite, which unifies all men.

Jesus said that love of God is the greatest commandment. "Thou shalt love the Lord thy God with all thy heart, and with all thy soul, and with all thy mind. This is the great and first commandment. And a second like *unto it* is this, Thou shalt love thy neighbor as thyself. On these two commandments the whole law hangeth." Divine love is such a transcendent thing that words describing it seem flat and stale. But words used in right understanding quicken the mind, and we should not despise them. Affirming that we do love God with all our heart, with all our soul, with all our mind, and with all our might will cause us to feel a love we have never felt before. No better treatment for the realization of divine love can be given than that which Jesus recommended.

Jerusalem, the Holy City, represents the love center in consciousness. Physically, it is the cardiac plexus. Its presiding genius is John the Mystic, who leaned his head on the Master's bosom. We establish the ruling attitudes of mind throughout our body by our daily thoughts, and they may or may not be in harmony with Principle. Our dominant thoughts about love will show forth in the heart center and establish there a general character. The loves and hates of the mind are precipitated to this ganglionic receptacle of thought and crystallized there. Its substance is sensitive, tremulous, and volatile. What we love or what we hate builds cells of joy or pain in the cardiac plexus. In divine order it should be the abode of all that is good and pure.

To be in subjection to the higher Power is the highest goal of human attainment. The spirit of obedience is the spirit of love. Love is the most obedient thing in the universe. It is also the greatest worker and will accomplish more for our happiness than all other faculties combined. If you want a servant that will work for you night and day, cultivate divine love. At times there may be obstacles in the mind that interfere with this fellowship of love. One of them is the thought that we owe our neighbor something besides love. For some wrong, fancied or otherwise, we think we owe him punishment. The higher Power tells us that we owe him love only, and by sending him the word of love the law is fulfilled, and the barrier is burned away. We must make friends with everybody and everything in order to have this mighty worker, love, carry out for us the divine law.

When we even faintly realize the love of God we begin to love our fellow men. There is a fervent love among Christians that is not found among any other group. Love is a divine ordinance, and those who let the love of God pour itself out in charity do truly cover and forgive a "multitude of sins," not only in themselves but in others; love pours its balm over every wound and the substance of its sympathy infuses hope and faith to the discouraged heart. Divine love has a balm for every ill.

The World Calls to Courage

Chapter 6

OVER NINETEEN hundred years ago a man taught a religion that changed the whole trend of thought of people. His teachings were called "the Way."

In the beginning He had few followers. He was, like Socrates, accused of treason and killed. His enemies took for granted that after His death His doctrine would utterly disappear, as had many doctrines before His time. However, they lacked spiritual discernment, for the teachings of the man Jesus of Nazareth possessed an element that the people vitally needed and they soon sprang up in regions far beyond the little land where they were promulgated; they spread to many lands and have been spreading ever since.

It was the Word of God that Jesus was teaching; the Word of God is the creative agent, and spiritual man is its supreme creation. Moreover, the man Jesus stands far out in front, as evidenced by His teachings. He is the divine man of this race. We should impress this on our consciousness. We should study His teachings. We should understand and follow them.

Jesus taught that the world belongs to man and that man is responsible for it. The human family is responsible for the poverty or the prosperity of the world. By our mental beholding and working we determine whether we shall have or have not.

In the days when the Israelites were held in captivity by the Babylonians, a few of the companions of the prophet Nehemiah were allowed to return with him to Jerusalem and to rebuild the wall. They engaged those remaining in the city to help; the Bible says "the people had a mind to work."

Our prosperity is the result of work—not physical work alone, but first mental and spiritual work. There is an everlasting marching on in every industry and science. We are never content with the present methods but are constantly seeking better ones; we are not content with our schools but are always finding easier ways to gain knowledge for ourselves and our children. Our nation is, therefore, progressing.

We find that Christianity is surprisingly progressive, too. Our religion is constantly unfolding new possibilities, new powers, and new beauties; we are on the way to a great outpouring of spiritual development. We have not realized what a wonderful religion we have. It is filled with possibilities, and these possibilities are made known to us in mind and spirit.

But we need more courage to develop these possibilities. We need more initiative. We need more awareness of this divine power in us and when we awaken to the spiritual man, which every one of us has within us, we shall see that through spiritual unfoldment all good things are possible of accomplishment, as Jesus promised.

All things are possible to us, only we must believe. Believe what? We must believe in ourselves, in this innate spiritual man in us and we must encourage him. Encourage him with what? With sound words, with affirmations of almightiness; then we shall have the key to the overcoming world.

Our most important study is our own mind, not only the intellectual mind but the spiritual mind. "Know thyself" was inscribed on the temple of Apollo at Delphi; and it must be inscribed on our own temple, "over" the door of our mind. "Know thyself." We must become acquainted with our own mind.

Now that it is being universally taught that with every thought our brain sends vibrations into the surrounding atmosphere, every progressive metaphysician is admitting that with this invisible thought stuff we are constantly making structures for ourselves and the world about us. The scientific world is also beginning to recognize the fact that man has within himself the capacity to re-form the world about him.

Modern metaphysicians have discovered that with every thought we think there is a movement of active forces—not only a movement of those forces, but a movement of everything connected with our consciousness, our body, our world.

Every time we speak we cause the atoms and

cells of our body to tremble and go through certain changes. Not only do we cause the cells and atoms of our body to form new adjustments, but we even affect the cells of the bodies of those with whom we associate.

We are told that "the desert shall . . . blossom as the rose" and that we shall have a millennium here on earth; that things will be changed "in the twinkling of an eye." This is a Biblical view. We find that changes come gradually, and they come through work.

We find in the Old Testament the poems and prophecies of Isaiah. He tells in the language of the Orient some of the signs of the millennium—and they have been shown by modern science!

> The wilderness and the dry land shall be glad; and the desert shall rejoice, and blossom as the rose. It shall blossom abundantly, and rejoice even with joy and singing; the glory of Lebanon shall be given unto it, the excellency of Carmel and Sharon: they shall see the glory of Jehovah, the excellency of our God.
>
> Strengthen ye the weak hands, and confirm the feeble knees. Say to them that are of a fearful heart, Be strong, fear not: behold, your God will come *with* vengeance, *with* the recompense of God; he will come and save you.
>
> Then the eyes of the blind shall be opened, and the ears of the deaf shall be unstopped. Then shall the lame man leap as a hart, and the tongue of the dumb shall sing; for in the wilderness shall waters break out, and streams in the desert. And the glowing sand shall become a pool, and the thirsty ground springs of water: in the habitation of jackals, where they lay, shall be grass with

reeds and rushes. And a highway shall be there and a way, and it shall be called the way of holiness; the unclean shall not pass over it; but it shall be for *the redeemed.*

In every generation since the dawn of history have been prophets who claimed that they received revelation of the end of the world. It is claimed that even Jesus told of the end of the world. However, more recent and accurate translations of the New Testament show this to be an error. What Jesus spoke of was "the completion of the age."

A vivid description of the end of the earth's civilization is found in the 34th chapter of Isaiah. Whether Isaiah knew any more about the end of the world than many modern prophets is a question.

History testifies to the fact that they are all wrong. The world is not coming to an end. Geologists say that it has taken the Colorado River at least fifty million years to carve out the Grand Canyon. It is logical, then, to conclude that God has a future for a globe that has taken Him so long to make.

But through poets, prophets, and pessimists in every age we are warned of what, from a human, destructive viewpoint, might occur. Shakespeare says:

"These our actors.
As I foretold you, were all spirits, and
Are melted into air, into thin air;
And, like the baseless fabric of this vision,
The cloud-capped towers, the gorgeous palaces,
The solemn temples, the great globe itself,

Yea, all which it inherit, shall dissolve;
And, like this insubstantial pageant faded,
Leave not a rack behind."

Now what we want to ask is this: Are these prophecies of the end of civilization and the destruction of the earth and all things the result of sane thinking or are they the work of sick minds?

They are undoubtedly the work of sick minds. The sane man with a little logic would determine that our God, with the power and wisdom to create a world of such mighty possibilities, would not destroy it and leave the destiny of all the good people to the mercies of a few unscrupulous fanatics.

The destiny of the earth and of its people is in the minds and hands of those who seek to know God as Spirit, and those who seek Him must seek Him in Spirit.

Jesus points the way, and by following His formulas we shall find the solution to every problem. All the formulas given by Jesus are constructive rather than destructive. He does not teach death but life. "If a man keep my word, he shall never see death."

Where in Jesus' teachings shall we find a formula to offset, to dissolve, to meet and nullify the atomic bomb? We find it in the 10th chapter of Luke and the 22d chapter of Matthew. This is the formula:

"Thou shalt love the Lord thy God with all thy heart, and with all thy soul, and with all thy strength, and with all thy mind; and thy neighbor as thyself." "This is the great and first commandment," Jesus told the lawyer who asked Him what was the "great" commandment. This is the fulfillment of all commandments.

The formula has been tested, and history shows that it has built and sustained civilization and produced peace, happiness, and prosperity.

Let us all join in prayer to this end, that we may take the formulas that Jesus gave as working principles, that they may be sent out in the world through the power of the word.

"Be strong and of good courage; for thou shalt cause this people to inherit the land."

Conscience

Chapter 7

THERE IS A divine goodness at the root of all existence. It is not necessary to give in detail the place of abode of each sentient part of this central goodness, for it is there, wherever you look, and whenever you look. No man is so lowly but that at the touch of its secret spring this divine goodness may be brought to light in him. Even the animals exhibit its regulating and directive power. This goodness sleeps in the recesses of every mind and comes forth when least expected. Many stifle it for years, maybe for ages, but eventually its day comes, and there is a day of reckoning. This is the law of universal balance—the equilibrium of Being. It cannot be put aside with transcendental philosophies or metaphysical denials any more than it can be smothered in the forces of the blind passions.

Men and women are loath to admit that there is within them a monitor with which they have sooner or later to cope, and they put off the day of reckoning as long as possible. They do not like to deal with this leveler of Spirit. It is too exact; it wants justice to the very limit.

Whoever has felt the prick of conscience has been spoken to by the Holy Spirit. Whoever has sat at the feet of his own inner convictions has been aware of God's presence.

Man is never without a guide, no matter how loudly he may be crying out for leading. There is always at hand a sure torchbearer if he will but follow the light. It is too simple, too easy! Man has formed in his mind a far-off God who talks to him from some high mountain in invisible space. By thus looking afar for his God he ignores the spark of divinity shining in his own being.

Herein is man fooled into believing that he can do the things that are not in harmony with his ideas of goodness and yet escape the consequences. He presumes that God is too far away to behold his shortcomings and he loses sight of the fact that God is right with him every moment.

This is the meaning of the old saying that a man and his conscience are good friends as long as the way is smooth, but when it grows rugged they fall out. They fall out because man has reached a point where he begins to consider his ways and he looks carefully over the life he is leading. This brings him to a beholding state of mind. He sees that what he considered right in the clear light of divine good is not up to standard. Here the divergence takes place between man and his conscience. They were friends in appearance only before or during the period of license. The conscience may seem to assent to the derelictions of man, but it is ever the inner protestant that keeps knocking at the consciousness until the steps are arrested.

Worldly fortune is not always a blessing to man.

In fact, under present customs it is apt to be just the reverse. As long as questionable methods are successful in bringing results, conscience has but a small chance for a hearing. It is only when failure follows the efforts of the misguided that conscience gets his ear. Then the field is surveyed with the eye of a general defeated in an unjust cause. The heat of battle blinded him, and he gave no thought to the lives he was uselessly sacrificing.

Here remorse gnaws the vitals of the unwise, and here the true wisdom is revealed. It is said that experience is a dear school, and only the wise learn therein. This carries with it its own nullification, like many of the intellect's wise observations. Experience is the school of fools. The truly wise do not take lessons within her doors.

There are two ways to get understanding. One is to follow the guidance of the Spirit that dwells within, and the other is to go blindly ahead and learn by hard experience. These two ways are open to everyone. It is recognized by the man who has had experience that he can advise the one who has not and thus save him the laborious steps of that rocky road. In the light of omnipresent intelligence, is there not One who knows all things, all roads, all combinations, and what will be the outcome of every one?

Do not men and women by their constant efforts to peer into the future prophesy a wisdom that knows all future? They certainly do, and when man looks in the right direction he always finds such an oracle.

It is the prerogative of Spirit to know the future, and when man consults Spirit with pure heart and unselfish motives he has pointed out to him the very lines his life shall be cast in if he is obedient to his most high God.

It is no great achievement for one who follows the leading of Spirit within to forecast the future. To Spirit the future is a succession of events based on the ideas revolving in the mind at present. Whoever rides into his own ideal realm can read his future for himself. He finds there a chain of causes at work that he can easily see will produce certain results. It is not necessary for him to read the definite line along which each separate idea will travel to its ultimate. This is the method of reasoning from cause to effect. In Spirit, cause and effect are one. They appear as one, and the ultimate is just as clear as the inception. In mind, all things reach fruition the very instant they are conceived. Time not being a factor, how can there be a beginning and an ending? The architect plans a house and sees it finished in his mind before a single stone is laid or a pound of earth excavated. He can change his plan many times before the construction commences. He can destroy it entirely if he so desires. So man builds the house of his own conscience. If he has been planning to build a home for himself alone, in which there is but one room, he created in mind just such a plan, and it is complete and awaits its coming into visibility. If he has made a plan of a larger structure, in which are many rooms, this plan will also come into visibility.

Some persons build their houses far ahead in mind and say nothing to anyone. Such persons make very substantial plans, which are infused with the most enduring substance of the invisible. Such were the plans of Napoleon when he silently determined to be emperor and of the shepherd who resolved to be Pope. Vanderbilt's rule of life, to which he attributed all his success, was to reveal his plans to no one.

Jesus said, "Let your speech be, Yea, yea; Nay, nay." Talking is a waste of energy—a dissipater of power. If you want the greatest success, do not talk too much about your plans. Keep a reserve force of new ideas always on hand as a generative center. Let your work speak for itself.

The electrician recognizes a certain universal law of action in the revolutions he builds into his dynamo. The energy produced is based on the size and texture of the dynamo and the rapidity of its motion. Mind has a law of dynamics equally as scientific. The character of an idea is the estimate of its size, and one's active faith in it determines the rapidity of its motion. Ideas generate energy with a swiftness unparalleled in physical dynamics. Rather than moving inanimate things, they move men and women. Rather than temporarily lighting our streets for a few hours, they light the lamps of intelligence that burn eternally.

The secret of doing this successfully lies in knowing how to handle our ideas. The electrician constantly improves the efficiency of electricity by studying the machinery that generates the power. The same rule holds good in mental dynamics. We must study our ideas if we want to improve the service of our body, of our intelligence, and of our surroundings, for from these ideas flow forth the currents that move the machinery of all of them. If our ideas are based in Truth and we are satisfied that they will stand the test of the most rigid justice, we do not want to let the currents they produce in our mind leak away on some grounded wire.

The world is full of people who are filled with high and mighty resolves to do good, and they are sincere, but they are connected with grounded wires. We must keep our wires properly insulated, or our plant will not prove successful. For instance, we are holding an idea of health, which is generating currents in our mind that might flow out on the wires of faith and heal the world, but we have broken the current by believing that it should pass through a pill, a magnetic hand, or the mind of someone who we think is stronger than we. We must stop all this and send our idea of health straight to the mark on the wires of our own true word. We have an intuitively correct idea of the truth on every question that comes to our mind, but we do not trust the idea. We impede its free currents by believing that some book, some person, or some church organization has sifted the truth and somehow established it before we came into existence. This fallacy makes a menial of the genius and puts out the light of the world in the minds of generation after generation of sons of God. Spiritual ideas must have spiritual wires, or their power dissipates. So we need to watch both the ideas we hold and the words with which we set them free. If we have an ideal world in which we see things as we want them, yet think it an impossibility that that world may be realized here and now, we are dissipating the power that our ideas are generating. So throughout the category of thought generation, every idea must have a wire that corresponds to its circuit or current. Our words, our acts, and our whole life must be in accord with our ideas.

The realm of ideas is at the call of each of us; it is, in fact, the source from which we draw our real sustenance. It exists in Being as universal intelligence. Since it is the cause and source of all intelligence, sooner or later it must assert its unobstructed sway in the lives of all mankind. When this realm of ideas becomes so active in the consciousness that it attracts our special attention, we call it a quickening conscience. It is the universal intelligence of Being asserting its inherent moral equilibrium. Man cannot always distort the fair face of the God-Image, whose likeness he is. He may for a season wear the grotesque mask of the mountebank or the fool, but in God's own good time he will be unmasked by that silent inner self that must be heard when its hour has come. God is not mocked, nor is the secret place of the Most High in every heart forever made a cave for thieves.

When conscience cries out in your heart, "Make straight the way of the Lord," you will save time by heeding it. Let its cleansing waters of denial flow over you. Change your ideas. Be meek and lowly. Let your thoughts go up to the Christ Spirit. Acknowledge Him as one whom you, in your mortal consciousness, are not able to comprehend in the majesty of His spiritual understanding.

If you are of haughty domineering, self-sufficient will, you stand as Herod, the ruler of Judea. You are married to the passions of the human soul. These passions lead you into sense gratifications so deep, so degrading that you cut off the head of the conscience that would have turned you into the highway of good. But the reign of the sense man is short-lived. Your kingdom is taken from you, and you are banished from your native land. This was the fate of Herod after he beheaded John the Baptist. This is the fate of everyone who refuses to listen to the voice of his higher self.

The key to the development of Jesus of Nazareth's great powers was in His meek and lowly submission to the Father. He disclosed this when He said, "Blessed are the meek: for they shall inherit the earth." Whoever makes himself nothing in the presence of God may be possessor of all things below God.

Man is open to God when he wills to be open. This opening is made by our attitude of absolute mental humility in the contemplation of spiritual realities. Thus, the likeness takes on the express image of the Father, and in no other way can it be done.

"I am meek and lowly in heart," said the mighty Nazarene. "Not as I will, but as thou wilt," was the mental attitude He always took when communing with the Father. It was always in the same spirit of love and willing obedience to the guidance of a wisdom that He knew transcended His own.

Jesus did not take the universe on His shoulders by affirming His self-sufficiency. He unloaded every burden and rested in the all-sufficiency of the Father. "I can of myself do nothing"; "the Father abiding in me doeth his works." This is the total denial of self—the giving up of all personal desires, claims, and aims. Before man can do this successfully he must change his ideas—there must be a mental house cleaning.

The command, "If any man would come after me, let him deny himself . . . and follow me," is not broadly interpreted by the world. Some men think that self is denied sufficiently when they acknowledge God as mind, life, love, substance and all else as error; others think that they have only to give up the recognized sins of the world and believe in a personal Saviour, Jesus. But the denial of self goes deeper than all this. To be effective, it must reach the very depths of the consciousness and dissolve all the organic forms that the ideas held by the personal self have there precipitated. Every human body has its stratified layers of consciousness. These strata have, like the earth, been built up layer after layer through ages and ages of sidereal time. The body we live in is the result of a labor that we began millions of years ago. It is the stored-up memories of our experience in thought generation. We may have dissolved that body ten millions of times, but no part of its reality has ever been lost to us. Because we have failed to energize it to the perpetuation of its form indefinitely is no argument against its being the very body we have had for aeons upon aeons. The form of it changes, but the mental pictures we have formed in all those ages are intact somewhere in our own private gallery.

But now the clouds are clearing away from our world, the "sun of righteousness" is rising with "healing in its wings." We are awakening to our powers and possibilities as sons of the Most High.

The day of selflessness has come. This day delivers us from all our burdens. We find that we do not have to bear any of the cares of existence on our shoulders. We say with Jesus, "All things have been delivered unto me of my Father." We do not breathe for ourselves, but rather God breathes in and through us. We do not have lives of our own, but we feel the life of God surging through all our organs. We say to our feet, our hands, and every part of our body, "You are now one with God; you are perfect in His sight." We do not think and speak by ourselves alone; we think and speak God's thoughts after Him, which rush through our mind like a mighty wind. Then tongues of fire come upon us, because we are inspired by the Holy Spirit. Neither do we have possessions of our own nor cares nor troubles about our life or our families; we leave all these things to God—we are absolutely without responsibility when we have fully denied ourselves and followed the Christ. All responsibility drops from us when we let go of the idea that we are personal beings and possessed of parts, passions, and faculties that belong to us individually. Nothing like a personal man exists in the idea of God. The idea of God is Jesus Christ—one universal man. Men are but the mind organs of that one man—they do not possess of themselves anything whatever, but all that the Christ possesses flows through their consciousness when they have ceased to believe in personality. This is the at-one-ment—"I am in the Father, and the Father in me"—and the apprehension of that at-one-ment dissolves forever that inner monitor called accusing conscience.

Man

Chapter 8

GOD IS PRINCIPLE; Christ is the idea of principle as it is brought into creation, and man is that creation on its way to the perfect expression of the Christ.

This being true, man must learn that he has within himself all the potentialities of Being. When this tremendous truth is revealed to him he sometimes forgets that his potentialities are to be expressed according to plans inherent in Being and he proceeds to make his world after his own design.

This is the first step in the fall of man—the belief that he can act wisely without first knowing the plan of God.

This fall takes place in his own consciousness. He follows the dictates of the animal nature rather than those of the higher wisdom, and in indulging them he eats the fruit of "the tree of the knowledge of good and evil," which is a consciousness of nakedness and separation from God.

Man is Being in miniature, and all the powers of God are available to him. These powers and possibilities are made manifest through man. It therefore follows that man is a most important factor in creation. It also follows that he should become acquainted with his part of the work and do his very best to carry it forward.

All the powers of Being are summed up and concentrated in the one word *I*. All possibility lies in this one word, and from it issues forth everything that appears. From the standpoint of the visible universe this I is man, and by reason of his divinity he makes and unmakes as he wills. At work with the powers of Being, man is the transformer of all things. In this lies his greatest strength and his greatest weakness.

The ego of itself is possessed of nothing; it is a mere ignorant child of innocence floating in the mind of Being, but through the door of its consciousness must be passed all the treasures of God.

How small, how insignificant is man—yet again how mighty, how important, how powerful. As Jesus truly said, "I can of myself do nothing"; "all authority hath been given unto me in heaven and on earth."

As this I, this man, comes into consciousness of the life, love, and wisdom of God, it builds for itself a consciousness; it begins to say "my" and "mine."

This is selfhood, the son taking his inheritance and going into a far country. But the Father does not condemn selfhood. In His eyes the son who stays at home and the son who exercises his freedom are equal. If the Father is free to do as He wills, the same privilege must be the son's inheritance, else he would not be "the fulness of the Godhead bodily."

Ignorance as to his place in Being and the powers

delegated to him is the one great giant that keeps man from his own. If he would acknowledge God in all his ways, in every thought and act, there would be revealed to him a new world, an undiscovered country lying all about him, ready for his occupancy.

This is the promised land that God reveals to those who are willing to be led by Him out of the bondage of ignorance, which is termed Egypt.

Egypt exists in the consciousness of every man, but his I AM does not have to remain in that dark place. God calls him up out of that animal condition in which his desire is for "pottage," and invites him into "a land flowing with milk and honey."

Whoever answers that call is guided by the Spirit of God; it may be through seas of error and deserts of wasted possibilities, but if he is faithful to that inner wisdom, he is finally led to the Jordan of demonstration and through it into his promised land.

But the real man is not flesh and blood; he is not body and brains. These are but his outer garments. Man is just as undefinable as God. The I within you is as great a mystery as the infinite I. You are just as great a mystery to yourself as you are to others. You do not conceive of your possibilities, nor can the most high archangel conceive of them. You are just as fully the son of God as was Jesus or any other Christlike man who ever existed. The I AM is the same in all men and all women. It is without limit in its capacity to express the potentialities of God.

Why, then, are you not doing the works of Jesus? Simply because you have not taken advantage of your privileges.

The way is open to you as it was to Him. All things are provided for you in the great storehouse of Being. You have but to go about getting them in an orderly way.

This "way" is revealed by the Spirit of wisdom, the Spirit of truth, which Jesus said the Father would send in His name. This Spirit of wisdom has always existed. Jesus did not create it, nor was it created for His special benefit, but through His demonstrations of an inner and higher power than men had been accustomed to, He opened the way into their consciousness for this Spirit of wisdom. They saw His works and "believed on him," and this belief made it possible for the Spirit to come to them.

This Spirit of wisdom is right now a part of the consciousness of everyone. It is in you and about you, and you will come into conscious relations with it when you believe on it and its powers.

If you ignore it and thereby deny that it exists in you and for you, you remain in the darkness of ignorance. It is exactly as if a man lived in the basement of a large house and refused to go upstairs, declaring that because the upper rooms did not come down to him they were not there.

You are to "go up . . . and possess" this promised

land. It is yours all the time, and you live in the world with it, yet you do not choose to see it. "The light shineth in the darkness; and the darkness apprehended it not."

Great is man; great are his privileges.
"I said, Ye are gods,
And all of you sons of the Most High."

Great is man; great are his privileges. But he must realize his spiritual nature before he can reap its benefits.

"Ye are not in the flesh but in the Spirit, if so be that the Spirit of God dwelleth in you."

So long as man is not conscious of the Spirit of God, he is in the flesh; that is, he is conscious of his body and its material surroundings only. This is the carnal consciousness that does not know God.

But it is man's privilege to rise out of this animal plane onto the spiritual plane and thereby come into an open communion with the Father and know as Jesus knew and have all the powers that He had—and greater ones.

Man is I. By itself I is potentiality only; associated with its cause, it is all-comprehensive.

God is life, love, Truth, substance, wisdom. Man is the potential I that recognizes these inherencies of Being and makes them manifest.

Wisdom, life, and substance are incorporated into man's consciousness as spirit, soul, and body; each takes form in him according to his recognition of it.

If man takes cognizance of body only, he becomes a mere living, breathing, eating, drinking animal. He lives in the flesh, and through his ignorant use of its full privileges he perverts it to the most base ends. He builds up within its pristine purity lustful images, and in carrying them to fulfillment in act and deed he fills the world with disease, discord, selfishness, poverty, and death.

If man rises a step higher and takes cognizance of mind as well as body, he cultivates the ambitions of the intellect and the lust for power. Government, commerce, art, and literature become his ruling stars, and he is not always careful about the means that he uses to attain his ends.

It is when he recognizes his supremacy over both these and abides in the inner Spirit, the Father within, that he finds his true estate and shines forth the image and likeness of the Most High, which he truly is.

The question is frequently asked, "Why, if God is perfect and man is His likeness and image, should there be imperfection in man?" The answer is that there is no imperfection in man. He is perfect potentiality proving itself. In the course of bringing forth this perfection there are processes he must go through. Life and intelligence are factors entering into this process of man's manifestation and they seem to fall short of accurate consummation in certain stages of the work. This, the limited consciousness, looks on and pronounces it failure. In a sense it is error, as is the boys' assertion that two plus two equals three. When, however, the correction is made and the work proceeds according to the principle, success is always the ultimate result.

When man fails to submit the impulses of the lower nature to the analysis of the higher, he is beguiled by the serpent and eats of the tree whose fruit is a concept of good and evil.

Man never indulges in his animal nature without having a reaction of discomfort, which he sees is opposed to that which is comfort. When this is extended into the experiences of a race the reaction takes on the aspect of good and evil. Thus, man in the Adam consciousness has come to look on the world in which he lives as subject to two opposing principles, which he has named God and Devil. When he discovers that principles are the basis of existence he pronounces these opposing appearances good and evil.

The so-called principles of good and evil are nonexistent outside the sense mind. The true God cannot be known to the sense consciousness, and whoever postulates a being who is good or not good, according to his sense concepts, is building a "man of straw."

Man is made in the image and likeness of God, and when he seeks to know himself he will find the true God and will know that he is one with Him.

God is life, and man is life. But life in its essence and life as seen in the living are not identical.

The sense man looks on living, moving things and says, "This is life." It is not life, but only the evidence of life. Man may know the life that is back of the living. When he feels the thrill of that life within him he has touched the divine energy that changes not.

God is substance, but not that which the sense mind perceives and calls matter. Material things are but the evidence of the substance that God is, and not the unchangeable foundation of Deity. God is intelligence, but not that shifting opinion which the sense mind calls intelligence.

Hence, to know the nature of Him whose image and likeness he is, man must detach his I from the Adam consciousness and attach it to the Christ consciousness. Then he will learn the meaning in the steps in creation that preceded him in the divine planning. Then he will learn that he is not a "worm of the dust" but that with God he is helping to form the divine plan of existence, which ever rests in Being.

Man is the executive power in Being and only through his willing co-operation can the designs of the true God be carried out. These designs are based on principles that cannot be changed, and man must come into such close touch with the wisdom of God that he will consciously co-operate in bringing the perfect creation into existence.

Man is the will of God externalized or projected into visibility, and this will must respond to the slightest impulse of the divine power within the depths of his own being.

The sense mind has long been the realm of man's labors, and it has truly made him earn his bread by the sweat of his brow.

In this realm he has formed a center of consciousness, which is termed the will. This seeming will must be given up, and the pure will must find its rightful place in the realm of God-Mind. Jesus was passing through this dissolution of the false will when He cried out, "Not my will, but thine, be done."

So each of us must become so obedient to the Spirit of God within himself that the image and likeness which he is will shine forth in its pristine glory and the sons of God take their place in the Father's house.

The Philosophy of Denial

Chapter 9

A GREAT NUMBER of things that you look on as realities are simply transient shadows that can be dissipated into nothingness by your telling them the truth as to their unreality.

The one cause, the unmanifest mind, from which springs all manifestation, is Principle whose inherencies are potentially perfect. Like the principle of mathematics or of music, it enters not into error or discord. "Thou . . . art of purer eyes than to behold evil." That is, Principle is supreme good, absolute substance, mind, life, love, intelligence. Its ideals are like it, perfect. The Christ man or true man is the perfect ideal, and humanity is that ideal on the way to realization. The ideal man, the perfect man of Divine Mind thus appears in the process of manifestation as subject to the conditions produced by his conscious thinking.

Although potentially perfect and incapable of producing a single condition of permanent consciousness out of harmony with divine Principle, many persons are impregnated with a belief of limitation, and they need the dissolving power of denial to set them free. By and through the imaging power of thought man can produce illusions that confuse him. This occurs only when he fails to look to Divine Mind for the source and nature of his ideals. Obviously, many are deceived into thinking that they are indeed bound, and the unhappy conditions claimed do show forth in them. This is only consciousness entangled in its own effects. We know that pure mind cannot be subject to lack in any form, and that which so appears must in some way be a departure from creative Mind.

It is an axiom in physics that action and reaction are equal. Thought is the working power of mind; it is mind in action. Your ancestors thought that which was not in harmony with the All-Good, and their thought showed forth in their bodies and affairs. You have admitted the error, and you must deny it in order that your consciousness may be restored to its clear, spiritual perception.

Denials may be made in many ways. It is not always necessary to say specifically, "I deny so and so." The conscious acknowledgment that you have been incorrect in your conclusion is denial. Refusing to entertain longer any thoughts of a sensual nature is denial. Withdrawing mental sustenance from low ideals is denial.

There is but one Mind, and we can deny away error conditions for one another. For instance, you have a patient who is in the consciousness of fever. You acknowledge to the mind of perfect serenity that there has been a departure therefrom, and that peace is now restored. The acknowledgment by you that there is but one universal Mind, and that your clear consciousness of this frees everybody and everything from sin and sickness, will release you, or another you hold in thought, from any belief you may have reflected. Jesus said, "Father, forgive them; for they know not what they do."

If you are not at all times conscious that God is the source of your being, and that He is universal justice, purity, peace, wisdom, and love, you wander from your course and are aware of danger, you are dashed upon the rock of selfish personality. Then you give way to a fit of anger or jealousy; you lust after the flesh, or envy your neighbor his possessions. "We have sinned [gone into error, fallen short], because we have forsaken Jehovah."

You cannot have consciousness without thinking. It is the nature of mind to think; your every thought, no matter how trivial, causes vibrations in the universal ether that ultimate in the forms of visibility. You know that the working power of mind is thought and that through thought all the conditions that seem to encompass you were formed.

If consciousness departed from Principle and formed images that were manifested as disease, discord, any limitation of the perfect, is it not possible for that same consciousness to undo its faulty work and build anew according to wisdom's plan? It certainly is, and we know by experience that when guided by the Spirit of truth, or Christ within, our consciousness rebuilds the weak and tottering structures of materiality and vivifies them with an undying energy and life.

You have been deceived into believing that you were born of fleshly parents, and that you are subject to the peculiar mental and moral trials and physical ills of your ancestors. The Spirit of truth, which is, yesterday, today, and forever, pure perfection, and which is now present in you, sets you free from this delusion.

You have been deceived into believing that mind is subject to matter. You have been told that the brain produces thought, and that mind is evolved from matter. You have not taken these claims right home to your own innermost intelligence and thought about them logically. Now that your identity as mind, as invisible unconditioned spiritual substance, is made clear to you, these surrounding delusions are cleared away. You now say daily and hourly, "All authority hath been given unto me in heaven and on earth."

You have been deceived into believing that there are those among your associates who are your mental, moral, or social superiors; that they have by acquired or conferred authority the right to dictate to and to influence you in matters religious, social, or moral. But the meek and lowly yet dignified and all-wise Spirit within you now burns with its own clear light, and you henceforth understand that you are one with the supreme mind that knows only original thought—that is influenced by nothing outside of itself. This is Truth, and the Spirit of truth in you now flames forth in acknowledgment.

You have been deceived into believing that you have certain traits of character to which you are bound by nature, and through them are confined or hampered in life. You may suppose, for instance, that you are naturally timid and fearful, therefore nervous and unfitted to face the world; or that you are cold and unsympathetic; or that you lack language or expression for your ideas; or that your memory is poor; or that you lack perfection in some other way.

Now these illusions crumble into nothingness, and your clear consciousness recognizes its own. At the center of the mind of every man is the light, the white light of Spirit. Fan to a flame this white light at the center of your being by proclaiming your identity with Christ. The salvation of the world rests with those who join Him and thereby bring peace and good will to all men. When the light of Christ comes to any man, it does not confine its rays to his consciousness alone but those who sit in darkness and negation see and feel its power.

You now know the law of righteous thinking that will bring you into a consciousness of your perfect dominion. Life is worth living because you can surround yourself with your highest ideals. Henceforth you are to keep in mind the consciousness of your spiritual origin. Now that you know your being is pure transparent mind, you can intelligently deny any undesirable trait and center your consciousness on the perfect Spirit within.

We have been burdened too long with the rubbish of antiquity. Cast it out of your consciousness and assume the mental dominion that was yours before the worlds were formed and you were one with the consciousness of the Father.

The same Holy Spirit that glorified Jesus, and through which He overcame the world, is now right here with us. It is here awaiting our recognition. It will cleanse our mind of all beliefs of heredity if we acknowledge its presence and power. Bathe yourself in this boundless ocean of wisdom, love, and light by holding for a few moments in the silence the thought:

"Thy Spirit sets me free:
Thou, only, healest me."

You are not afraid when your consciousness is centered in the principle of good. You know that God is all; that there can be no opposing power. The plague and pestilence do not then reach you, for you have nothing in common with the cause that brings them about.

Man ought never to show forth sickness, poverty, discord, or death, and he never would have done so had his consciousness remained in its primitive relation to cause.

It is now dawning on the consciousness of those who in these latter days listen attentively to Spirit, that, when understood in its right relation, even the form symbol or body will take on the appearance of immortality. Consciousness will become so intensely alive and so thoroughly at one with the supreme life that the form idea, which is potential in mind, will reflect bodies whose perfection will be divine. Many are now coming into an understanding of the law that will ultimate in their physical translation, like Elijah, in chariots of fire. This does not come under the head of the miraculous, for if history is to be credited, many in the past went through this change; and as God is Principle and "no respecter of persons," we should expect at any time a recurrence of that which has been. Progressive men in the ranks of physical science are being led by analogy to the conclusion that this is a possibility. Edison said that his investigations had convinced him that atoms are centers of intelligence; that the human body being composed of atoms (each of which is an intelligent entity), a man could, by getting control of these atoms through the will, live forever.

This is the legitimate outworking of perfect Principle—the steady onward march of mind from stage to stage in the unfoldment of its infinite possibilities. In the harmonious working of life's problems according to Principle, there are no backward steps.

"God is *not the* God of the dead, but of the living," said the illumined Jesus. The God of the living is always present with you, awaiting your conscious recognition. Let the divine life substance flow into your mind, and it will cleanse you of all false race beliefs. You will become renewed in thought and in action; your face will again show forth the freshness of youth, and immortal life will be written upon your brow.

When your consciousness rests in Spirit, your dominion is sure and certain; then you do not come under the law of denial. You can simply conform to the command, "Be still, and know that I am God," and the work is done.

The Affirmative Word

Chapter 10

CHRISTIAN metaphysicians have discovered that man can greatly accelerate the formation of the Christ Mind in himself by using affirmations that identify him with the Christ. These affirmations often are so far beyond the present attainment of the novice as to seem ridiculous, but when it is understood that the statements are grouped about an ideal to be attained, they seem fair and reasonable.

When one understands the power of words spoken in spiritual consciousness the results are in fulfillment of divine law.

The affirmation of any good statement of Truth puts us in conscious contact with the Christ Mind and quickens and releases the light and energy stored up in the subconscious mind; then the process of redemption begins.

Should we pray in words that imply faith in a sure answer to our prayer, or should we ask meekly, leaving the answer to the will of God? This proposition confronts most of us at various times. Our mind wavers between the two attitudes, and the answer is always weakened by the wavering whether we realize it or not.

Whichever way we decide to pray, we quote Scripture to fortify our position and usually find enough to satisfy us that we are right. The majority of the prayers of Jesus are affirmations, according to English translations, which are not always in harmony with the original text. For example, the great Lord's Prayer, which we so universally use, in the original is a series of affirmations. The translators had no conception of the majesty of the Son of God, and they twisted His prayers of decrees into a supplication for help. When we realize that we are the outlet of a mind that seeks an adequate expression, we shall cease our begging prayers and elevate our thoughts and words to the high standard set by the Master.

God created man to express Him in the manifest world, and we fall short in our mission when we fail to measure up to our divine authority. Jesus, the Son, affirmed, "All authority hath been given unto me in heaven and on earth." When He prayed things happened, and He expected His followers to do likewise. We are asked why our prayers do not always bring things to pass, as His did. The usual answer is that we have not developed faith or assurance equal to that of Jesus. But how shall we go about developing this Christ faith? We have asked for the faith of Jesus and even declared it in His name, yet it does not abide with us continually. Why?

The answer is that we have not realized and appropriated our princely heritage. We have not trained our mind away from the negative race beliefs but have allowed it to fall into the popular channels of thought, thereby attaching ourselves even more firmly to human impotency. Here is a point of which every Christ initiate should be made aware, namely that the Christ baptism gives us a very decided mind expansion and infuses into our thoughts and words a power that we did not before possess: "His word was with authority."

Jesus taught His followers to assert the affirmative in thought and word. We do not know the exact words He used in His statements, but judging by the English into which they have been translated from the Greek, Jesus was very positive in His assertion of the power of spiritual man, and especially of those who follow His teaching. He taught and demonstrated that the word can be used to build or to destroy. The destructive power was illustrated in the fruitless fig tree. It was in this connection that He laid down the laws through which we can bring forth whatever we desire. What could be stronger in this respect than the following statement? "All things whatsoever ye pray and ask for, believe that ye receive them, and ye shall have them."

The universal life current is subject to the word of man. This current flows into and through man's body from above as Spirit through the sympathetic nerves and from below through the motor nerves as life energy. In Genesis the flow of this current is symbolically described as "the tree of the knowledge of good and evil" and "the tree of life."

Jesus said, "Ye are from beneath; I am from

above." In our present race consciousness we affirm and identify ourselves with the objective consciousness or tree of the knowledge of good and evil. By acquiring the ability consciously to go within and affirm our unity and power in Spirit we can gain control of the tree of life current and live forever. Certain occult schools teach the power of the will to lay hold of the tree of life current and increase its flow to hundreds of years. But if the objective consciousness is not redeemed from its thoughts of evil, no permanent good will be attained. Adam was put out of the Garden of Eden because of the possibility that he might eat of the tree of life and live forever in his ignorance and sin. The regeneration taught by Jesus and carried out in each soul by the Spirit of truth is the only safe and sure way to eternal life.

The greatest need of the human family is thought control. Here is a great truth. However, thought control is weak if the mastery of the two currents that animate the body is ignored. Jesus' words were filled with power because He had mastery of the lower life current through His realization of the Spirit from above. He said, "The words that I have spoken unto you are spirit, and are life." He gripped the current from above and united it with the one from below, producing a supermind voltage. The most potent point of contact of these two currents in the body is in the larynx, the music box of the mind. The voice can be made strong and vibrant by one's centering the attention at the nerve complex in the larynx and affirming, "*All power is given unto me! All power is given unto me!*" This not only gives power to the voice but also changes the negative waters of life into positive elements of energy. This process was illustrated when Jesus turned the water into wine at Cana in Galilee. This early miracle in His experience took place in His body, forming part of the regeneration. The name *Cana* means "place of reeds" and *Galilee* means "rolling energy" or momentum, indicating what takes place in the larynx when words are spoken. When the words are spoken with spirit, not only conditions without are changed but the watery cells of the body are transformed from sluggish action to "wine" or a state of high positive activity. If thoughts of a destructive character dominate, the body suffers and eventually disintegrates. Thus we are judged by our words.

We who have studied the mind know from our experience that the ills of humanity all have their root in thought and the failure of man to express his thoughts in harmony with Principle.

Thought control is imperative, and there is urgent need of teachers on both the mental and spiritual plane of consciousness if the race is to go forward in development. To this end there needs to be more co-operation between the two planes of consciousness, because they complement each other. Religion becomes practical and effective in everyday life when it incorporates psychology as part of its litany. Without religion psychology is weak in its fundamentals, and without psychology religion fails to give proper attention to the outlet of its ideals. The fact is that religion, comprehended in its fullness, includes psychology. Jesus was a profound psychologist.

The fact is that religion cannot be effectively taught in its scientific aspect without application of the higher attributes of the mind. Paul teaches this most effectively, and none other comes anywhere near him in this respect. He says, "Have this mind in you, which was also in Christ Jesus." He refers repeatedly to the Mind of Christ as the model for all Christians. In Hebrews we are told, "I will put my laws into their mind."

Comparing our mind with that of Jesus, we find many points in which we can improve ourselves in thought and word. We may assert that we believe, but do we prove it in our mental deportment? Every Unity reader may become a disciple and reap the benefits promised by Jesus if he will assume the mental attitude of a Christian and practice the power of words.

Spiritualizing the Intellect

Chapter 11

We have no independent mind; there is only universal Mind, but we have consciousness in that mind and we have control over that consciousness. We have control over our own thoughts, and our thoughts make up our consciousness. By analyzing ourselves we find that we unconsciously separate ourselves into different personalities. We should do this work consciously. We should enter into the understanding that the I AM power is given to us in consciousness, and then join or unify that consciousness with the great Christ Mind.

Thus the central idea in this word affirmation that we are seeking to understand and to incorporate into our consciousness is the Christ Mind. As spiritual metaphysicians we find that the Christ Mind is the Mind of Spirit. In the consciousness of man it functions as two states of consciousness: one in the flesh, the other in Spirit. But Spirit is the source of all.

In daily worship it is well to impress on the sensitive mind that it is unified with Divine Mind through Christ or the same mind that was in Christ Jesus.

With this understanding as the basic principle of our thought, and realizing the power of thought to impress itself on the sensitive plate of man's mind, this prayer is invaluable:

I separate myself in consciousness from the mind of the flesh, that I may enter into the mind that was in Christ Jesus.

First we disentangle our thoughts from the flesh and lift them up to Spirit. We hold them steady in spiritual consciousness until they begin to get hold of Spirit essence, Spirit power, Spirit love. Everything that we see in the manifest world comes from this one Spirit-mind; so it is well to hold this affirmation until the most sacred ethers respond to our realization:

I separate myself in consciousness from the mind of the flesh, that I may enter into the mind that was in Christ Jesus.

In connection with the value of prayer and realization we call to mind the experience of Jacob and Esau in receiving the blessing of their father Isaac.

It was customary to give the first-born the prior blessing, and this blessing of the first-born belonged to Esau. But Jacob through connivance with his mother Rebekah, got the blessing, and of course it was by subterfuge. The procedure was dishonest. Esau was wroth against his brother Jacob for taking precedence in this case, and threatened his life. The mother advised Jacob to flee to the country of her brother Laban, and Jacob immediately set out on his journey. He was, however, in a wilderness of thought.

As metaphysical Christians we take this Scripture to be a spiritual history of man as well as a history of outer events. We try to read it according to the meaning. Spiritual things must be spiritually discerned. The Bible is a spiritual book. We arrive at a greater understanding and enhance our interest in these two different characters, Jacob and Esau, when we look on them as representative not only of individuals but of the race as a whole.

If we study the characters Jacob and Esau, we find that they represent dominant ideas in man, ideas that pertain to his very being. They are of vital interest to us. As we read out of the law we find that Esau—a hunter and a lover of the things of appetite—represents the flesh, the body. A man of a little different turn of mind, one who loved home and the quiet, spiritual things of life, Jacob represents the mind, the intellectual man.

Of course in the process of evolution the natural man comes first. Then the spiritual man begins to unfold in us. But here we find that the spiritual man, or rather the intellectual man illumined by Spirit, gets the blessing. The Israelites set great store by this blessing. Rightly understood, blessing is a great source of inspiration. It lays a firm foundation in the mind and it brings out the good. A curse emphasizes evil; a blessing emphasizes only good. Thus we come into an understanding of the importance to the soul's evolution of the development of these two characters, Jacob and Esau.

As we look at the blessing that Isaac gave Jacob and Esau (for he did bless Esau after he had blessed Jacob, giving Esau the blessing that would bring out his character), we discover that he was governed by law. The blessing he gave Jacob belonged to the mind and not to the body; in fact, it belonged to the part of the race mind concerned with service, the part that has to do with the exercise of authority.

In this blessing there is a calling forth of the inherent faculties of the mind that enter into the exercise of authority: "Let peoples serve thee." The mind dominates the body. "Let . . . nations bow down to thee." We see nations being dictated to by some great mind, some great dictator.

"Let thy mother's sons bow down to thee:
Cursed be every one that curseth thee,
And blessed be every one that blesseth thee."

Here we can see the power of ideas to bless or to curse. We see that he who uses his mind to curse gets the curse in return, while the mind that blesses receives blessings in return.

If we study our mind we find that they are radiating energy constantly and that whatever we send out comes back. We see this in evidence everywhere, not only individually but collectively.

To Esau Isaac said,

"Behold, of the fatness of the earth shall be thy dwelling,
And of the dew of heaven from above;

And by the sword shalt thou live, and thou shalt
serve thy brother."

Here in these symbols we have the body man or man of the flesh. "The fatness of the earth shall be thy dwelling": man lives very close to the earth. "And by thy sword shalt thou live": he is the man of flesh that the man of the mind sends forth to carry out his warring ideas. Intellectual man is the general or the governor or the dictator that sends the man of the flesh to do his bidding.

"And it shall come to pass, when thou shalt break
loose,
That thou shalt shake his yoke from off thy
neck."

In the evolution of man, the body (Esau) finally comes into its own. The Isaac blessing is carried out in the world today. We find that the working classes that have been under the yoke of the intellect—the intellectual man—now are beginning to assert themselves. They are breaking loose from the yoke of bondage of the intellect, the mind; the flesh is beginning to assert itself. We are giving more attention to the flesh every day. People are awaking to the fact that the body is an important part of man, and so we see everywhere the fulfillment of this blessing. If we study ourselves, we find a tendency toward the working out of the two minds. The tendency of the intellect is to dominate, to have its way and ignore the body. But the body is beginning to break loose from this bondage and demand its own. It is saying to us: "Why, I am a very important part of this world. You can't leave me and go off to some faraway place. I am an important part of you." So with Esau the flesh begins to break loose from this dominance of the mind that has separated it from the good things of the heavenly estate. We raise it up, and it begins to become a power in the world.

We must soon come to a place in our social and economic evolution where the earth and all that it has will be recognized in a larger way, and become an integral part of our life. This is very clearly taught in this story of the mind and the heart. Isaac (the I AM) recognized this unity and brought it into expression in his blessings of his two sons. We have these two sons, the mind and the body. It is the mind that connects us with Principle. Jacob made this connection, but Esau had as yet failed to come to the place where he could recognize that he was a son of God. Jacob took that blessing from him. He became the sole representative when he was really the secondary one, but he forged ahead in the race, and today we have the intellect dominating almost everything. It is evident that the Jacob faculty (the illumined intellect) has assumed its prerogative in the world today. The illumined intellect rules. God is omnipresent, God is intelligence, just as much in the mind as anywhere. The blessing of the I AM consciousness brings out the intelligence that has the greatest ruling power. But we find also that we must bless not only the body but everything connected with it.

As we study the Bible we find that after he broke away from the material consciousness Jacob had many experiences. He went into another country, another state of consciousness, in which he was awakened spiritually to a still higher plane. In the 16th verse of the 28th chapter of Genesis we read: "And Jacob awakened out of his sleep, and he said, Surely Jehovah is in this place; and I knew it not." He was in the sleeping state of consciousness. He had a dream and saw a ladder extending from the earth up to the heavens and angels or messengers of God ascending and descending. Jehovah was at the top of this ladder and told him that he was to be the father of a great nation and that a certain blessing was to be poured out upon him. When Jacob awoke he saw that God was in that place; that the place was the very "house of God," the dwelling place of God. In other words, here was evidence of omnipresence.

Each individual must have his first awakening to the truth that God is everywhere and that, regardless of surroundings, God is omnipresent Spirit-mind. In this instance Jacob was surrounded by rocky hills, and he piled up stones and made an altar to Jehovah right there in the desert. The great lesson for us is to know that God is everywhere evenly present, no matter how material the surroundings may seem to be. To the unregenerate man there is usually a great awakening in an experience of this kind.

When man begins to see beneath the surface and realize that God is functioning with him constantly, he seeks to make a union with infinite Mind, omnipresent God-Mind. In the Scripture we read: "And Jacob vowed a vow, saying, If God will be with me, and will keep me in this way that I go, and will give me bread to eat, and raiment to put on, so that I come again to my father's house in peace, and Jehovah will be my God, then this stone, which I have set up for a pillar, shall be God's house: and of all that thou shalt give me I will surely give the tenth unto thee."

Here was a covenant or an agreement made by a man in his first great illumination on the subject of the one omnipresent substance. He may have realized before that God was the great I AM, the Jehovah leading him, but he had not realized that this earthly substance, the rocks about him, were really representative; that they are a part, a living part, of the God substance; that the I AM man in his illumination has a part in that substance; that it is his substance through infinite Mind. The covenant of Jacob to give one tenth of all his increase was the real meaning of what in modern times we call tithing, making God a partner in all our finances.

Jacob became a great financier of the ancient world, and through the illumination that he got from Jehovah he knew how to take advantage of every opportunity.

We do not take Jacob as an example of what man should do in his finances, for he was something of a trickster. He represents the world in its trickery and cunning in finances. But apparently Jehovah, the one Mind, was with him. (Sometimes there are contradictions that we cannot understand.) When we know that we are the directive power as regards all that belongs to us, we may get on financially; however, in the end we have to account to infinite Mind.

But with it all, Jacob loved Jehovah and shared his wealth with the Lord. He proved the law of tithing, that tithing is one of the foundation principles of financial increase. Man can become a great possessor of the substance of this world if he follows certain rules of tithing. Jacob gives us the key, which is the recognition that God is part of all substance, and that if man wants to handle substance wisely and well, if he wants to handle it for great financial success, he should do what Jacob did: take God into partnership with him.

There is an omnipresent financial Mind, and if man begins to deal with this financial Mind he will have a partner that has all resources at His command.

If you want to become a rich man, if you want to be possessed of every good thing in the world, take God as your partner, incorporate His mind into your mind, in your daily giving. Give of your substance with the thought that it is God's money you are handling. Realize that it is His tenth that you are giving for His glory. With this thought in your mind you will begin to attract new spiritual resources, and things will begin to open up in your affairs. You will know that infinite Mind is with you. This is what Jacob realized, and he became a greater financier. I would say to everyone who wishes to demonstrate prosperity: take God into partnership with you and you will demonstrate abundance.

Conscious Mind and Subconscious Mind

Chapter 12

WE ARE ALL well acquainted with the conscious mind. Through its use we establish our relations with the outer realm and recognize our individual entities. Indeed, there are some who claim that the conscious mind is the only mind there is. They are simply holding a thus far undiscovered country to be undiscoverable. Of such persons as these Cardinal Newman spoke when he said that they "are only possessed by their knowledge, not possessed of it." But in due season they will awake and respond to the call of Spirit to "come up higher."

The subconscious mind is the vast, silent realm that lies back of the conscious mind and between it and the superconscious. To one who does not understand its nature and its office, it is the "great gulf fixed" between his present state and the attainment of his highest desire, his good. The subconscious may be called the sensitive plate of mind. Its true office is to receive impressions from the superconscious and to reproduce them upon the canvas of the conscious mind. Man, however, having lost the consciousness of the indwelling Father as an ever present reality, has reversed the process and impresses the subconscious from the conscious mind. In this way the former is made to register impressions of both good and evil, according to the thought held in conscious mind at the time the impression is made. And since it is the purpose and the nature of the subconscious mind to reproduce, or to throw upon the screen of the conscious, the exact impression that it has received, the conscious mind is thus made to express two sets of opposing ideas. No enduring structure can be built by one who is "a double-minded man, unstable in all his ways."

Man must go back to his Source and let its clear light flood his whole being with Truth. He must lay aside forever the idea of serving two masters and must look to the one Master, even Christ, the spiritual consciousness within. Jesus said that He came not to destroy the law, but that the law might be fulfilled through Him. It is the mission of every man born into the world to fulfill the law of Being; one can do this work only by working from cause to effect.

"Be subject therefore unto God . . . Draw nigh to God, and he will draw nigh to you." It is a comfort to know that we do not have to make the entire journey alone back to the Father. We read that when the prodigal son was coming back to his father, "while he was yet afar off, his father saw him, and was moved with compassion, and ran, and fell on his neck, and kissed him."

The superconscious mind is ever ready to pour

forth the divine blessing, quick to respond to the call of the conscious, which it meets on the middle ground of the subconscious. Spirit is omnipresent, but man has hedged himself about by a world of illusion of his own creating, and through its mists he cannot see the Father, or catch the light from the superconscious mind. Jesus came to give us conscious control of the intelligence and the power necessary to dispel these mists, in order that "the true light, *even the light* which lighteth every man, coming into the world," might shine full upon us. Thus we see that the superconsciousness sends its rays of intelligence and power first into the consciousness, and that through their influence man is led to seek the kingdom within, where all things are added to him.

The superconscious mind lifts up, or regenerates, both the subconscious and the conscious, transforming them into the true image and likeness of God. The conscious mind must be faithful during this transformation. It must look ever to the superconscious for all direction and instruction. It can of itself do nothing with assurance, because the Spirit of wisdom rests in the superconscious.

The subconscious exists for the benefit of the conscious mind, but unless regenerated it thwarts the efforts of the conscious at every step, so that "ye may not do the things that ye would."

The subconsciousness is sometimes called memory. One whose subconscious mind has not been systematically trained, or awakened, is often heard to say that he has "a poor memory." Sometimes he tries to recall a word or a name that he knows "as well as he knows anything," but he cannot speak it. Several days later, perhaps, when there is no longer any desire to recall it, the word "comes to him." The subconsciousness has reproduced it, but the process has been slow.

The subconscious mind can be trained by the conscious to work systematically and reliably, but the conscious mind must be faithful and consistent in creating the impressions that it seeks to make upon the subconscious.

For five years after learning typewriting a stenographer used the sight method. Then the advantages of the touch system (typing without looking at the keys) were impressed upon her and she desired to learn that system. At first she did not believe that she could do it, because she was so "used to the other way" and was engaged in active work, with no time for practice. But the desire continued, and before long an opportunity came. She obtained a different position, where there was leisure for practice. She had daily association with an enthusiastic student of the touch system and she was encouraged in every way. For about six months she devoted her conscious mind to remembering the keyboard and to controlling the movements of her fingers. Eventually the subconscious mind was so impressed with a knowledge of the right movements and the right positions of the fingers that it regulated them of itself.

"Thought is quicker than vision" was her motto during the tedium of practice, and she has proved it to be true. If she strikes the wrong key she knows it instantly without having to look at her work, and she has been heard to say that her fingers express her thoughts much better than her tongue, because they have had so much attention and such persistent drill. Of course, the fingers can do nothing of themselves, because mind is the only actuating power.

The subconscious mind is also known as the heart, and the many references to it in the Bible show that its nature and its office were well understood by the writers of Scripture. "Keep thy heart with all diligence; For out of it are the issues of life," indicates the importance of the proper development of the subconscious mind. Man cannot, however, keep his heart, or control the expressions from his subconscious mind, without the aid of Spirit. The superconsciousness reaches to the depths of the subconscious and sets free the energies bound in error thought; that having been done, man can easily reach and mold the subconscious, in harmony with divine ideas. The regeneration of the subconscious is not the work of the conscious, but of the superconscious mind acting in harmony with the conscious.

The Spirit of God, speaking through Ezekiel, commands, "Cast away from you all your transgressions, wherein ye have transgressed; and make you a new heart and a new spirit." This command is to the conscious man, or mind. But later the Spirit of

God says, "A new heart also will I give you, and a new spirit will I put within you," thus signifying that the whole mind must be embraced in the regeneration. There must be perfect co-operation of the three phases of mind in order to produce the perfect man. "I, Jehovah, search the mind, I try the heart, even to give every man according to his ways, according to the fruit of his doings." "Purify your hearts, ye double-minded," says James. We purify our heart when we turn conscious attention within and the pure ideas of the superconscious mind come forth to meet our call. "He that is joined unto the Lord is one spirit." When we seek the superconsciousness and make conscious connection with it we harmonize all the forces of mind and body; we lift up the subconscious until a complete, conscious unification of the three phases of mind is affected and we become established "in singleness of . . . heart." We can say with the Psalmist, "His heart is fixed, trusting in Jehovah." We fear nothing, for we know that we draw on the divine ideas in God-Mind and that they all are good.

Reincarnation

Chapter 13

THE WHOLE MAN—spirit, soul, and body—must be lifted up into the Christ consciousness of life and perfection, which is the goal of man's existence.

The Western world in general looks on re-embodiment, or reincarnation, as a heathen doctrine. Many people close the door of their minds to it, without waiting to find out what message it may bring when interpreted in the light of Truth. It is the object of this article to set forth the Unity teaching concerning reincarnation; to show why we consider it reasonable and to explain its relation to, and its place in, the Christ doctrine.

The teaching of Jesus is that all men shall, through Him, be made free from sin and be saved to the uttermost—spirit, soul, body. But until this salvation is attained, there is death. To give men opportunity to get the full benefit of salvation, life is necessary, and a body through which to express life is also necessary. So, when man loses his body by death, the law of expression works within him for re-embodiment, and he takes advantage of the Adam method of generation to regain a body. Divine mercy permits this process in order that man may have further opportunity to demonstrate Christ life. But generation and death must give place to regeneration and eternal life. The necessity of rebirth must, therefore, pass away with all other makeshifts of the mortal man. It will have no place when men take advantage of the redeeming, regenerating life of Christ and quit dying.

Re-embodiment should not be given undue importance, because it is merely a temporary remedy to be followed by the real, which is resurrection. The whole man—spirit, soul, and body—must be lifted up into the Christ consciousness of life and perfection.

Jesus teaches that rebirth or reincarnation is the unifying force of nature at work in its effort to restore man to his original deathless estate. Man, through his disregard of the law of life, brought death upon himself, as taught in the 3d chapter of Genesis. But a single span of life, from the birth of an infant to the death of an old man, does not constitute all of man's opportunity for living. Life is continuous and in harmony with the wholeness of Being only when it is expressed in a perfect body; hence man must have a body in order to gain an abiding consciousness of life. Through repeated trials at living, man is finding out that he must learn to control the issues of life in his body.

The objections that the natural man raises to re-embodiment arise largely from the fact that he lives in the personal consciousness and cannot see things in the spiritual and universal. He thinks that by re-embodiment he loses his identity. But identity endures. Personal consciousness does not endure. The personal man is not immortal, and he dies. This is clear to anyone who is willing to give up his belief in the reality and importance of the personal consciousness.

The personal man with all his limitations, all his relations, must give way to the universal, the Christ man. The privilege is ours to give up or forsake everything—father, mother, husband, wife, children, houses, lands—for Christ's sake and so enter into the consciousness of eternal life. By doing this we come into the realization of eternal life and receive a hundredfold more of the very things that we have forsaken. If we refuse or neglect to make this "sacrifice" and prefer to live in the narrow, personal way, and cling to the old personal relationships, there is nothing for it but to meet the result of our choice, and to sever all those relations by death. It is just a question of giving up a little for the all and gaining eternal life. So if re-embodiment frees one from the old, personal relationships, it is not such a dreadful thing after all, for it gives us new personal relationships. Rising out of these into the universal is a work that everyone must do willingly for himself. Death and re-embodiment do not give redemption. Reincarnation serves only as a further opportunity to lay hold of redemption.

The pure, incorruptible substance of Spirit, built into the organism through true, pure, spiritual thought and word, makes the body incorruptible and eternal. As the mind changes from error to Truth, corresponding changes take place in the body, and the ultimate of these changes is perfection and wholeness in every part. Therefore those who are trying to lay hold of eternal life have ground for their faith in the promise that they will be saved from the grave.

Knowing that spirit, soul, and body are all necessary to man and that he cannot truly be said to live except in their conscious union and expression, the error of believing that death is the open door to a higher life, the gateway to heaven, is easily seen. There is no progress in death. Death is negation. The demonstration of eternal life can be made only in life—soul and body together working out the problem and together being lifted up.

Sense consciousness has no power to lift itself out of ignorance and sin, so the mere matter of repeated births has not taken the race forward. It is the descent of Spirit from time to time, as the people have been able to receive it, that has made all progress. As men's growth has made it possible, new truths have been discerned and new dispensations have come. When the time was ripe, Jesus came and brought the good news of salvation from death. But His words had to work in the race consciousness for nearly two thousand years before anyone was sufficiently awakened and quickened to believe in a complete redemption and to strive to lay hold of it. The promise is that the leaven of the Word will finally leaven the whole of the human family and that all people will come into the light of spiritual life.

From the standpoint of creative Mind it is plain that re-embodiment serves a purpose in affording opportunities for spiritual development. All that is gained in spiritual growth in one's life experience becomes part of the individual's real identity; and if he is faithful, he will finally gather such a store of spiritual power and wisdom that he can demonstrate salvation of his body through Christ, who is "able to save to the uttermost." But, we would repeat, reincarnation is only an opportunity.

"The hour . . . now is." Right now the resurrection work is going on, and men and women are awakening to a new consciousness of life, understanding, and bodily perfection. This resurrection work must extend to every member of the Adam race, whether he is what we call alive or whether he, as Jesus said of the dead, sleeps. All must be awakened and be unified in soul and body.

Many of the present-day ideas of resurrection have come down from past centuries of ignorance and have been accepted without question because they seem to be supported by a literal interpretation of certain Bible texts. But in these, as in all Scripture, we should go back of the letter and see the spiritual meaning of the parables and the symbols used to teach the truth about the raising of the dead. Thus we shall find unfolding day by day in ourselves the awakening and resurrection of thought that we once supposed would come in a single day to the bodies of those in the grave. When this raising of our dying and dead thoughts has gone far enough in us, we shall find ourselves gradually slipping into continuous health; that is, we shall realize that our bodies are self-renewing and therefore naturally immortal. Such a mighty and far-reaching work would be included in the promise "Greater *work* than these shall he [man] do."

Mention is also made in John's Gospel (King James Version) of "the resurrection of damnation." Damnation is condemnation. Paul makes it very clear that, by Adam's transgression, condemnation came on all his race. As death has no power to help anyone, the condition of the Adam man is not bettered by dying. Therefore, when people are re-embodied they "come forth . . . unto the resurrection of damnation," in other words, condemnation or correction. Everyone begins where he left off. But though one may have died in condemnation and been re-embodied in that state, he has opportunity, when re-embodied, to come up into Christ (in whom is no condemnation), identify himself with the Christ race, and demonstrate through Him the deathless life. So is proved the divine justice of including all in sin in Adam, that all may be delivered in one, even Jesus Christ.

Everyone who would demonstrate that he is risen with Christ must first lay hold of life by faith and affirm without wavering that he is raised out of sin and condemnation and death into eternal life. Then the word of life carries on day by day the resurrecting, redeeming work in the mind and in the body. "I die daily," I am raised daily. Every day some old limitation or error loses its hold and passes away and the imperishable, incorruptible substance of Truth becomes a little more firmly established in consciousness. In this way the body is transformed and raised up in honor, incorruptible, immortal. This is the raising of the dead, as commanded by Jesus.

However, some of the details of this great work must of necessity be, at this time, mere speculation. It is not profitable to allow our minds to dwell on mortal questionings about how the work of Spirit is to be done in and through us. It is our place to hold ourselves in a positive life thought, realizing always the omnipresence and perfection of life in God, thus bringing perfect life more and more into manifestation in ourselves and in others. When we realize how much our faithfulness means to the race, we shall rejoice in being true to the great principles of Truth that will bring to pass the time when death and the grave will be no more. "And death shall be no more; neither shall there be mourning, nor crying, nor pain, any more: the first things are passed away."

That you do not remember your past lives proves nothing. Neither do you remember the day on which you were born, but you do not on that account question the fact of your birth. Comparatively little of your present life is remembered, but this does not alter the fact that you have lived. Memory, to the natural man, is a matter of physical brain records, photographic or phonographic in character. The memory of experiences in past lives is not clearly recorded in the new brain structure of the infant. Such memories are usually in the nature of vague impressions; the sense of identity is blurred. But in the book of life, the great mind of the universe, all identity is sharply marked, and as the individual becomes quickened and raised out of personal consciousness into the universal, he will be able to bridge over the breaks in personal experience. He will come to himself. Realizing his spiritual identity as a son of God, he will not entangle himself with either present or past personality, but will claim and demonstrate his divine sonship. He will no longer limit himself to a brief span of life, beginning with birth and ending with death, but will live in the consciousness of eternal life, which has neither end nor beginning.

God's Abundance

Chapter 14

TIMES OF DEPRESSION bring out the fact that in days of prosperity man either forgot the prayers and struggles that brought him to success and apparent safety, or else he failed to build his fortune on a firm financial foundation. If he had thought more about the source of life and substance, he would have escaped the needless grind of the poverty he has endured right here in the midst of abundance.

There is both a primary and a secondary law of increase. Men pile up possessions by human effort, interest, and other ways of secondary increase, and grow into the thought that these are the real means of attaining prosperity. But possessions gained in this way rest on a very insecure foundation and are often swept away in a day. Then men are in despair and often think that their means of existence is gone forever and life is not worth living. Such persons are really never happy in their wealth, because there is always a lurking fear that they may lose it. They are secretly troubled with the thought of lack, in the presence of worldly plenty.

We cannot help but think that a wise and provident Creator must have planned more permanent possessions for His offspring. In Truth, He has so planned. Access to this permanent source of all man's good lies in his power to possess and mold in thought the omnipresent substance of Spirit.

Apparently we live in two worlds: an invisible world of thoughts, and a visible world of things. The invisible world of thought substance is the real world, because it is the source of the world of things, and man stands between the two, handing out with his thoughts the unlimited substance of Spirit. When man gets understanding of the right relation between the visible and the invisible into his mind and active in his thought, all his needs will be met. That is what Jesus meant when He said, "Seek ye first his kingdom, and his righteousness; and all these things shall be added unto you."

But the invisible thought substance provided for man is very sensitive to man's thought about it; that is, about the things that originally came from it and that man claims as his possessions. If man hoards the things that he seems to possess, he clogs the spiritual channel from which they originally flowed and so receives sparingly from that source.

Watch your thoughts when you are handling your money, because your money is attached through your mind to the one source of all substance and all money. When you think of your money, which is visible, as something directly attached to an invisible source that is giving or withholding according to your thought, you have the key to all riches and the reason for all lack.

Paul had a consciousness of this law of thought

in finances when he wrote to the Corinthians, "He that soweth sparingly shall reap also sparingly; and he that soweth bountifully shall reap also bountifully."

This law of the mind affecting resources applies especially to those who are responsible for the temporal needs of the family, because they are seriously interested and put actual thought substance into the monetary income and outgo. Children and those who have not labored to gain money put very little thought substance into it or its spiritual idea. But the heads of families need thought discipline in raising the prosperity consciousness, because the law is no respecter of persons and millions of good people, the very salt of the earth, are in want the world over because they do not know this law of sowing and reaping in thought. The financial field is a large one, and we are all sowing and reaping in it every day. The financial genius deals in large transactions because he has large ideas of supply.

God, being the giver of inexhaustible ideas of plenty, loves those who abandon themselves to a cheerful state of mind so that He may pour more abundance into their thoughts. Then Paul says, "God is able to make all grace abound unto you; that ye, having always all sufficiency in everything, may abound unto every good work."

The thought behind a gift is the real measure of its value and efficiency. Jesus illustrated this when He called the attention of His disciples to the poor widow who cast two mites into the treasury, which was large in her estimation because it represented all her living. It is what we think about our gift that gives it spiritual value and not the stamp on the coin. This is illustrated by the story about the careless Scot who tossed a crown, thinking it a penny, into the collection plate, and when he saw his mistake asked to have it back. The deacon refused, and the Scot grunted, "Aweel, aweel, I'll get credit for it in heaven." "Na, na," responded the deacon, "ye'll get credit for the penny."

It is easy to forget that God is the source of our supply, so we have our days of thanksgiving and our grace at table, besides the discipline of acknowledging the supreme Giver of all good whenever we receive or pay out money. The practice of tithing is undoubtedly the most expansive practice in this respect, and thousands of successful businessmen use it to their continuous financial and spiritual profit.

Jacob began tithing very early in his successful career. "Of all that thou shalt give me," he vowed to Jehovah, "I will surely give the tenth unto thee." Tithing for the support of his religion was incumbent on every Israelite, and of all the races of the earth none other has equaled the Israelites in financial ability.

Metaphysical insight reveals why the Jews have always been noted for their prosperity. By the act of tithing, men make God their partner in their financial transactions and thus keep the channel open from the source in the ideal to the manifestation in the realm of things. Whoever thinks that he is helping to keep God's work going in the earth cannot help but believe that God will help him. This virtually makes God not only a silent partner but also active in producing capital from unseen and unknown sources, in opening up avenues for commercial gain, and in various other ways making the individual prosperous.

That the law works for those who persist in its application is beyond question. But nearly all who practice tithing confess that in certain stages of their prosperity they fall into the error set forth in Deuteronomy: "Beware lest thou forget Jehovah . . . when . . . thy silver and thy gold is multiplied, and all that thou hast is multiplied; then thy heart be lifted up, and thou forget Jehovah thy God . . . *lest* thou say in thy heart, My power and the might of my hand hath gotten me this wealth. But thou shalt remember Jehovah thy God, for it is he that giveth thee power to get wealth."

We give money a dignity that does not belong to it. Money and those who possess money are looked on as wielding a certain power, and we give them deference that in no wise belongs to them. The foundation of this is fear; we fear the power of those who use money to their own ends.

Various plans have been proposed to rob money of its power—or the power that men have given it—

the idea being that money is responsible for the abuses that have grown up through its use. But the destruction of money will not cure the evils that have come into being in the name of money. It is not money, but the love of money, that is the root of all evil. What men need to know is that money represents a mind substance of unlimited abundance and accessibility; that this mind substance cannot safely be hoarded or selfishly used by anyone; that it is a living magnet attracting good of every kind to those who possess it; that those who train their thoughts to depend on this mind substance for supply of all kinds never lack. When there is a need, they simply sing and pray and praise and give thanks that their need is bountifully supplied. If the mind is free from attachment to money or love of it, and lovingly concentrated on the divine substance, there is never failure in the demonstration.

"Because thou servedst not Jehovah thy God with joyfulness, and with gladness of heart, by reason of the abundance of all things; therefore shalt thou serve thine enemies that Jehovah shall send against thee, in hunger, and in thirst, and in nakedness, and in want of all things."

This was the admonition of Moses to the Children of Israel, and it holds good to this day. Making a living is a species of slavery to most persons. To them God is a slave driver, and they are continually under the lash of their own thoughts of how hard it is to make a living. Life to them is just one task after another without any hope of finding rest and peace.

This certainly is not the destiny planned by an all-powerful and all-loving Father for His children. When we groan and sweat under the stress and strain of life, we are serving Satan instead of God. The satanic consciousness would make us believe that there is a limited amount of the things necessary to life and that we must labor hard to get our share. It is true that such conditions do come upon those who have turned their faces from God. "In the sweat of thy face shalt thou eat bread."

However, those who follow Jesus in the worship of the loving Father escape the effects of the curse of the serpent and are restored to the liberty of the sons of God.

All work becomes divine for man when he affirms that he is working for God and that God is a generous paymaster. Then joy and gladness of heart will automatically spring up in the soul "by reason of the abundance of all things." This means that when we praise God and give thanks for His supply and support we open our mind to the inflow of the abundant spiritual essence of all things.

Jesus said that before we can enter the kingdom of the heavens we must become as little children. Most children are bubbling over with happiness. They have not yet been taught how to take life in the serious, solemn manner of the average adult. They hop and they skip and they sing, and their daily needs are met.

We all look back on the joys and freedom of our childhood and wish that they might have lasted always. And why not?

We have been taught that in mature life we have many hard lessons to learn, that trials and tribulations are an essential part of man's life, and that we must experience them in order to develop our character; that is, our consciousness. But Jesus said we must become as little children before we can enter the kingdom of heaven and that the kingdom is within us.

The little child has no consciousness of the tribulations of life, and the logical conclusion is that when we unload false states of mind and become childlike we shall begin to realize what heaven is like.

" 'For your Father knows your necessities before you ask Him. Consequently, ye must pray in this way:

" 'Our Father in the Heavens; Your Name must be being Hallowed;

" 'Your Kingdom must be being restored.

" 'Your Will must be being done both in Heaven and upon the Earth.

" 'Give us to-day our to-morrow's bread;

" 'And forgive us our faults, as we forgive those offending us, for You would not lead us into temptation, but deliver us from its evil.' "

This translation of the Lord's Prayer is found in "The Complete Bible in Modern English," by Ferrar Fenton.

In a footnote to this translation Mr. Fenton says:

> The above is the literal translation of the original Greek, retaining the Greek moods and tenses by the clearest English I could. The old versions, having been made from a Latin translation, could not reproduce the actual sense of the Saviour as given by the Evangelists, for Latin has no Aorist of the imperative passive mood used by Matthew and Luke.
>
> The force of the imperative first Aorist seems to me to be that of what is called a standing order, a thing to be done absolutely, and continuously.
>
> Ferrar Fenton says that the Aorist is a tense expressing complete action in a single movement. So we see that according to the preface of the Lord's Prayer as originally given by Jesus, He wants us not to pray for something to be done in the future. Instead, since God has already provided the things we need before we ask Him, our prayers should be in the nature of a command implying our recognition of the fact that they are now appearing in our world. As Fenton says, the prayer is of the nature of a standing order, "a thing to be done absolutely, and continuously."

So we see that we are not to beg God to provide for us, implying that He has been like an improvident parent whom we have to remind of His remissness. God has provided absolutely and continuously for every need of man, individually and collectively, and everything belongs to us: "All things whatsoever the Father hath are mine," said Jesus.

Faith-Thinking

Chapter 15

MAN CAN NEVER discern more than a part of the circle in which he moves, although his powers and capacities are susceptible of infinite expansion. He discovers a faculty in himself, and cultivates it until it opens out into a universe of correlated faculties. The farther he goes into mind, the wider its horizon, until he is forced to acknowledge that he is not the personal, limited thing he appears, but the focus of an infinite idea.

That idea contains within itself inexhaustible possibilities. These possibilities are projected into man's consciousness as an image is reflected in a mirror, and, through the powers vested in him, he brings them into manifestation.

Thus man is the most important factor in creation —he is the will of God individualized.

There is but one God, hence there can be but one ideal man. Each individual is the focus of the life, intelligence, love, and substance of this one universal man, Christ.

We draw all our substance, of whatever nature, mental or physical, from Him: "In him we live, and move, and have our being."

Our identity as individuals is formed by the infinitely various combinations of His attributes. We are the will of this Grand Man, Christ, and all of us draw on Him, through our sentient volition, for whatever we need.

All that any individual has ever expressed, or may ever express, is open to each one of us, because there is but one fount and we all stand as equals in His presence.

There is one principle of music; but there are millions of combinations, in symphony and song, of the few simple tones on which that principle is based. These tones are expressed in form as notes. They may be on the staff, in variations beyond computation, and similar variations may also be repeated above and below the staff.

So each one of us focuses the attributes of man in his consciousness in infinite combinations on the staff —the intellect; above the staff, the spiritual; below the staff, the animal.

Certain arrangements of dominant tones are recognized by musical composers as producing harmony. So in man; certain combinations of the attributes of the Christ in the individual, Jesus, produced the harmonious man, Christ Jesus.

We refer to the Christ as man, because our language has no word which expresses the two-in-one of Being. The Hebrew *Yeve* is a term that includes both male and female attributes.

Paul inspirationally said: "Have this mind in you, which was also in Christ Jesus: who, existing in the form of God, counted not the being on an equality with God a thing to be grasped."

This is the problem set before each one of us. We all want to know how to let the mind be in us which was in Christ Jesus. We feel the stirring of powers and capacities which we have never been able to use because of a weakness in some co-ordinating faculty.

One person may have a talent suppressed because of diffidence; another may have a talent rendered obnoxious by excessive egotism. This all shows that our powers are making servants of us. We must know who and what we are; we must take our place in the Godhead and marshal our forces.

There are various methods for doing this. Most of them are limited; they never get above the intellect; they do not venture into the spiritual. Most of the methods are theoretical; they are written down by those who have perceived the truth but have not carried it out in detail.

One man let his life be a demonstration of the bringing forth of the powers of the Christ; this was Jesus of Nazareth.

From within He gave forth the doctrine of the Christ; externally He stood for perfected humanity, Jesus. His apostles represented the powers of all men acting their respective parts under varying moods, but eventually blended into the one harmony—perfect man.

In order to command our powers, and to bring them into unity of action, we must know what they are, and their respective places on the staff of Being.

The Grand Man, Christ, has twelve powers, represented in the history of Jesus by the twelve apostles. So each one of us has twelve powers to make manifest, to bring out and use in the attainment of his ideals.

The most important power of man is the original faith-thinking faculty. Note particularly the term, "original faith-thinking faculty"; a great deal is involved in this definition. We all have the thinking faculty located in the head, from which we send forth thoughts, good, bad, and indifferent. If we are educated and molded after the ordinary pattern of the human family, we may live an average lifetime and never have an original thought. The thinking faculty in the head is supplied with the secondhand ideas of our ancestors, the dominant beliefs of the race, or the threadbare stock of the ordinary social whirl. This is not faith-thinking. Faith-thinking is done only by one who has caught sight of the inner truths of Being, and who feeds his thinking faculty on images generated in the heart, or love center.

Faith-thinking is not merely an intellectual process, based on reasoning. The faith-thinker does not compare, analyze, or draw conclusions from known premises. He does not take appearances into consideration; he is not biased by precedent. His thinking gives form, without cavil or question, to ideas that come straight from the eternal fount of wisdom. His perception impinges on the spiritual, and he knows.

To the question, "Who do men say that the Son of man is?" those who reflected the indefinite, guessing thought currents of the day, answered: "Some *say* John the Baptist; some, Elijah; and others, Jeremiah, or one of the prophets."

But Jesus is not asking for secondhand opinions; He appeals direct to the faculty in man that always knows. He says, "But who say ye that I am?" and that faculty represented as Peter, answers, "Thou art the Christ, the Son of the living God."

Then the Christ blesses him, and says: "Flesh and blood hath not revealed it unto thee, but my Father who is in heaven. And I also say unto thee, that thou art Peter, and upon this rock I will build my church; and the gates of Hades shall not prevail against it."

The thinking faculty in man makes him a free agent, because it is his creative center; in and through this one power, he establishes his consciousness—he builds his world. Through the volition of this faculty, he can refuse to receive ideas from Christ; he can cut himself away from the realm of original Truth or from the illusionary universe in which he is forever unraveling tangled ends and chasing shadows. Thus we see clearly that this faculty is the rock, the foundation on which our consciousness must be built.

For generation after generation, humanity had exercised the thinking faculty, and fed it on the illusions of sense, and "every imagination of the thoughts of his heart was only evil continually." The root of the Hebrew word here translated evil is *aven,* which means "nothing." Thus man was feeding his thinking faculty on nothing, instead of true thoughts from God.

As the result of this lack of conscious connection of the thinking faculty with the Fountainhead of existence, humanity had reached a very low state. Then came Jesus of Nazareth, whose mission it was to connect the thinker with the true source of thought. Thinking at random had brought man into a deplorable condition, and his salvation depended on his again joining his consciousness to the Christ. Only through that connection could he be brought back into his Edenic state, the church of God.

Then it was, in the darkness of intellect's night, that the thinking faculty caught sight of its higher self and joyfully exclaimed, "Thou art the Christ, the Son of the living God," and the response to that gleam of spiritual perception was the acknowledgment of faith as the foundation on which the church of Christ is built.

What an incalculable amount of time, energy, and effort has been wasted trying to build conditions of harmony, by both individuals and society, without making the connection between the thinker and the true source of thought.

If you have not recognized the spiritual center within yourself, and have not acknowledged allegiance to it, you are drifting in the darkness of sense.

You are allowing your thinking faculty to draw its thoughts (which are its food) from the chaos of ignorance, and you suffer the consequences in the discordant world it creates for you. Do not forget that everything that appears in your life and affairs, physically, mentally, or otherwise, has sometime been sent forth from your thinking faculty. It is only through the power vested in it that you can come into consciousness of anything. Consciousness makes your heaven and it makes your hell.

Some persons have let the thinking faculty run away with them, and they cannot control their thoughts. So some drivers let their automobiles run away, but the law always holds them responsible for damage done, and they find it cheaper in the end to give stricter attention to driving.

Get clearly into your understanding that you are not the faith-thinker, Peter. You are Jesus; Peter is one of your twelve powers.

Before this dawns on you, you are a carpenter; you are a builder in the realm of matter. Peter is a fisherman, one who draws his ideas from the changeable, unstable sea of sense.

When you realize that you are Mind, and that all things are originally generated in the laboratory of Mind, you leave your carpenter's bench and go forth proclaiming this Truth that has been revealed to you. You find that your tools in this new field of labor are your untrained faculties. The first of these faculties to be brought under your dominion is Peter, the thinking power. This thinking faculty is closely associated with another power, your strength (Andrew; Andrew and Peter are brothers), and you say to them, "Come ye after me, and I will make you fishers of men."

"Going on from thence"—that is, when you have trained these faculties until they are in a measure obedient, you discover two other powers: John (love) and James (justice). These are also brothers, and you call to them both at the same time.

You now have four powers under your dominion; these are the first apostles of Jesus. With these you begin to do the works of Spirit.

You now have the power to heal the many that are "sick with divers diseases, and cast out many demons," and to preach "throughout all Galilee."

That Peter stands today at the gate of heaven is no mere figure of speech; he always stands there, when you have acknowledged the Christ; and he has the "keys of the kingdom of heaven." The keys are the thoughts he forms, the words he speaks. He then stands "porter at the door of thought," and freely exercises the power that the Christ declares: "Whatsoever thou shalt bind on earth shall be bound in heaven; and whatsoever thou shalt loose on earth shall be loosed in heaven."

You can readily see why this faith-thinker, Peter, is the foundation; why faith is the one faculty to be guarded, directed, and trained. His words are operative on many planes of consciousness, and he will bind you to conditions of servitude if you do not guard his acts closely.

The people who let their thinking faculty attach itself to the things of earth, are limiting or "binding" their free ideas, or "heaven," and they thereby become slaves to hard, material conditions, gradually shutting out any desire for higher things.

Those who look right through the apparent hardships of earthly environments, and persistently declare them not material, but spiritual, are "loosing" them in the ideal, or "heaven." Those circumstances must, through the creative power vested in the thinker, eventually arrange themselves according to his word.

This is also especially true of bodily conditions. If you allow Peter to speak of erroneous states of consciousness as true conditions, you will be bound to them, and you will suffer, but if you see to it that he pronounces them free from errors of sense, they will be "loosed."

Until faith is thoroughly identified with the Christ, you will find that the Peter faculty in you is a regular weathercock. He will, in all sincerity, affirm his allegiance to Spirit, and then in the hour of adversity deny that he ever knew Him.

This, however, is in his probationary period. When you have trained him to look to Christ for all things, under all circumstances, he becomes the stanchest defender of the faith.

How necessary it is for you to know the important place in your consciousness that this faculty, Peter, occupies. You are the free will, the directive Ego, Jesus. You have the problem of life before you —the bringing forth of the Grand Man with His twelve powers.

This is your "church." You are the high priest without beginning of years or end of days, the alpha and the omega, but without disciplining your powers you cannot do what the Father has set before you. Your thinking faculty is the first to be considered. It is the inlet and the outlet of all your ideas. It is always active, zealous, impulsive, but not always wise. Its nature is to think, and think it will. If you are ignorant of your office—a prince in the house of David—and stand meekly letting it think unsifted thoughts, your thinking faculty will prove an unruly servant and produce all sorts of discord.

Its food is ideas—symbolized in the gospels as fish—and it is forever casting its net on the right, on the left, for a draught.

You alone can direct where its net shall be cast. You are he who says, "Cast the net on the right side." The "right side" is always on the side of Truth, the side of power. Whenever you, the master, are in command, the nets are filled with ideas, because you are in touch with the infinite storehouse of wisdom.

You must stay very close to Peter—you must always be certain of his allegiance and love. Test him often. Say to him, "Lovest thou me more than these?" You want his undivided attention. He is inclined to wander. We say our "mind wanders." This is an error. The mind never wanders. The faith-thinker, Peter, wanders; he looks in many directions. He stands at the door of heaven, the harmony within you; the same door has the world of sense on its outer side.

Peter looks within—he also looks without. This is his office, and it is right that he should look both ways. But he must be equalized, balanced. He must look within for his sustenance; he must recognize the Christ before he can draw his net full of fish.

Keep your eye on Peter. Make him toe the mark every moment. Teach him to affirm over and over again. Say unto him "the third time, Simon, *son* of John, lovest thou me?" He may say, "Lord, thou knowest all things; thou knowest that I love thee."

This is a very common protest. We hear in this day of modern metaphysics that concentration is not necessary; that it is only necessary to perceive spiritual Truth; that the demonstration will follow. Jesus gave us many lessons on this very point. He knew Peter like a book. He knew that this faculty was versatile but apt to change its base frequently. When in the exuberance of his allegiance Peter protested that he would lay down his life for Jesus, the Master said, "Verily, verily, I say unto thee, The cock shall not crow, till thou hast denied me thrice."

You must teach Peter to concentrate. Teach him to center himself on true words. It is through him that you feed your sheep (your other faculties). Keep him at his task. He is inquisitive, impulsive, and dictatorial when not firmly directed. When he questions your dominion and tries to dictate the movements of your other powers, put him into line, with, "What is that to thee? follow thou me."

Descartes said, "I think, therefore I am." This is precisely as if Jesus had said, "I am Peter, therefore I am." This is the I AM losing itself in its own creation. Exactly the converse of this statement is true: "I am, therefore I think."

Thinking is a faculty of the Ego, the omnipotent I AM of each one of us. It is a process in mind, the formulating process of mind, and under our dominion.

The I AM does not think unless it wills to do so. You can stop all sense thought action when you have learned to separate your I AM from the thinking faculty. Know this, and live in Christ.

Be no longer a slave to the thinking faculty. Command it to be still and know. Stand at the center of your being and say, "I and the Father are one." "I am meek and lowly in heart." "All authority hath been given unto me in heaven and on earth."

"I am, and there is none beside me."

The Appropriation of Divine Life

Chapter 16

GOD IS LIFE, and wherever the pulse of life beats, there God is. Man cannot give nor take life, but so long as he thinks he can slay the living and so long as he proceeds to slay either man or beast, he will be at enmity with life. Those who would lay hold on eternal life must seek in every way to preserve the forms in which it manifests.

We all have life, and it is God's eternal life, but it does not become ours in reality until we consciously realize it. The one who enters into eternal life, as did Jesus, must lay hold on that omnipresent life and make it one with his body. This is the secret of inheriting eternal life.

So long as man continues to lose his body through death he will be in doubt as to the reality of eternal life. Eternal life means to be eternally conscious of life in its fullness. By his very belief that life can go out of his body, man shows that he is not in the consciousness of eternal life. In theory he may see that life is omnipresent, and may reason to himself that he cannot therefore get outside of life, yet the appearance is that he lets it slip away from him. To entertain thought that life can even temporarily slip away will rob man of the consciousness of eternal life.

The remedy is: Lay hold on eternal life. Have compassion on the life in the body of every living creature, and especially in your own body. Declare life perpetually abiding in the organism. Erase some of the ways through which you are dissipating the life of your organism. Robbers are at work on your body every day. They are the lusts of passion and appetite. Resolutely drive them off. Give life the sanctuary of your present thought and pay the price of overcoming.

God is life, and they who worship Him must worship Him in the life consciousness; that is, in Spirit. When I worship Him in this way, I am vitalized immediately. In order to build up the real, permanent life consciousness I must touch the great inner life current. There is no other way.

The first step in the realization of life is always to know that God is life, abundant, omnipresent, eternal, and the second step is to make positive connection with God life by declaring oneness with it.

Within my body is the center where pure life is generated. This center is the fountain from which shall spring rivers of living water. When quickened by Spirit through faith in the indwelling Lord, the source of life, the waters of life are set free and purified.

By keeping my mind steadily on the pure, sweet, redeeming life of Christ, and refusing to allow any thought to come in that stops the consciousness of the universal life flow, I increase my power to appropriate more life, and every cell in my body thrills with the new life of Spirit.

Go in mind to the spiritual place that can be described only as I AM. When you touch I AM, it changes the whole course of your thought and your life. You are the offspring of God, of life. In life you live, move, and have your being.

In Scripture the divine life combined with divine substance is termed "the Lamb of God." This phrase carries the symbology of the lamb's purity, innocence, and guilelessness. Its nature is to vivify with perpetual life all things it touches.

The pure life of God flows into man's consciousness through the spiritual body. This is the "river of water of life, bright as crystal, proceeding out of the throne of God and of the Lamb," referred to in the 22d chapter of Revelation.

Jesus came proclaiming, "I am the way, and the truth, and the life"; "I came that they may have life, and may have *it* abundantly"; "I am the bread of life . . . which cometh down out of heaven, that a man may eat thereof, and not die."

The whole race groans waiting for the redemption of their bodies. Jesus gave us the one and only way to redemption, which is to incorporate the great I AM into our consciousness. "I am the resurrection, and the life." Make the resolve that you are master over all the life forces of your being. Do not look away off for help; you will never find it outside your own consciousness. God's power must be incorporated in your consciousness, and you must understand how it works and work with it. Through thought you must work Truth into every part of your body temple. This is not too difficult, but it requires attention and persistence. The body requires spiritual quickening, because it carries on a line of action beyond the realm of conscious thinking. If I live in a temple that belongs to me I should know what is going on in it.

The lifting up of the life forces and resurrection have the same significance. One who has discovered the Truth of Being is raised, lifted up in consciousness, resurrected daily out of old subconscious negative thought conditions into the one positive reality.

The body is the fruit of mind. Do not talk about the body as being a low vibration, or as material. In the study of mind action, take the body into consideration as the fruit of thought, and affirm that it is pure, holy, undefiled.

The life source is spiritual energy. It is deeper and finer than electricity or human magnetism. It is composed of ideas, and a man can turn on its current by making mental union with it.

The higher life is a higher state of mind. It exists as the soul of God; and you know it when you realize, *"I am the Son of God."* You bring this life into manifestation by acting from the divine life idea. The consciousness of eternal life places one in the stream of life that never fails.

Through repeated and constant affirmation in

mind of the one and only pure substance of God everywhere present, we change the life currents in the organism until the corruptible flesh puts on incorruption.

All the Way

Chapter 17

WHEN WE SING, "I'll go with Him all the way," we do not always realize the mighty import of our words. Jesus went all the way from the human to the divine. He went all the way to immortality. He raised not only His own consciousness from despair and hopelessness to assurance and confidence in the presence and continued help of a loving Father-God, but He opened the way for the whole race to do likewise. When we determine to follow Him all the way we undertake the mighty work of the ages, a revolution of character before which the famous tasks of Hercules pale into insignificance.

As a matter of fact no one has ever followed Jesus all the way in the revolution in our race thought that He initiated. Many devout, sincere men have attempted to do so, but Jesus is yet to be understood and imitated in His work of salvation.

In the first place we have not understood the depth of our bondage to error and evil, nor the enormity of the consequences if it is allowed to continue. But Jesus knew how the human mind wraps itself up in its own error thought and brings darkness and desolation beyond redemption, unless the light of divine understanding is released in the consciousness. Jesus knew how to quicken this inner light by being Himself the great Light, and He showed us how to attain the same spiritual brightness. In the face of ignorance, superstition, and persecution He boldly proclaimed: "I am the light of the world." "Ye are the light of the world." "Even so let your light shine before men; that they may see your good works, and glorify your Father who is in heaven."

To understand Jesus' experiences in their spiritual significance and their effect on our human bondage we should become better acquainted with the real character of the man and His relation to us, because the many claims of Jesus' spiritual superiority made by His followers and Himself must have a basis of Truth.

That Jesus had elements of greatness far beyond those of any other man that has ever lived on this earth is universally accepted by both the religious and the secular world. Some Christians claim that He came direct from heaven; that He was very God incarnate. Other Christians see in Him simply the fulfillment of the ideal man designed by Divine Mind. Neither of these views quite meets the logic of unbiased reason considered in connection with the events of Jesus' life.

If Jesus was very God and had all power, why did He suffer the agony in Gethsemane and cry out to His Father for help? If He was a mere man, an evolved representative of our race, why did He lay claim to an existence prior and superior to the Jesus incarnation, "And now, Father, glorify thou me with thine own self with the glory which I had with thee before the world was." "Before Abraham was born, I am."

He claimed the whole human race as His "flock" and compared them to sheep with Himself as the shepherd:

> I am the good shepherd; and I know mine own, and mine own know me, even as the Father knoweth me, and I know the Father; and I lay down my life for the sheep. And other sheep have I, which are not of this fold: them also I must bring, and they shall hear my voice; and they shall become one flock, one shepherd. Therefore doth the Father love me, because I lay down my life, that I may take it again. No one taketh it away from me, but I lay it down of myself. I have power to lay it down, and I have power to take it again. This commandment received I from my Father.

But they did not understand. "There arose a division again among the Jews because of these words. And many of them said, He hath a demon, and is mad; why hear ye him? Others said, These are not the sayings of one possessed with a demon. Can a demon open the eyes of the blind?"

Men in Jesus' time could not understand how what appeared to be an ordinary man could be the beginning of a whole new race of men as Jesus claimed to be. So they thought He was crazy when He made the assertion. We in our day do not fully understand how one man and one woman increase their species. It is a divine mystery, yet we bear witness to it.

In the 1st chapter of John's Gospel it is written:

"He was in the world, and the world was made through him, and the world knew him not. He came unto his own, and they that were his own received him not."

The fact is that the relationship which Jesus bears to the human family is quite beyond our present intellectual comprehension.

In order to understand the status of Jesus we have to visualize a universe like that in which we live as having existed during billions of years in the past, as having fulfilled its mission in the evolution of a superrace of men, and as then passing away leaving as its fruit God-men with creative power. Jesus was one of the God-men of that ancient creation, and it was His destiny to bring forth from the depths of Being a race of potential gods, place them in an environment where they could grow as He grew and become, like Him, a Son of God. As stated by Paul, "we are also his offspring."

The beginning of our race evolution is given in the allegory of Adam and Eve in the Garden of Eden. Jehovah is Christ, who formed man out of the dust of the ground and breathed into his nostrils the breath of life.

When the Adamic race reached a point in their evolution where they had personal-will volition, they began to think and act independently of the Jehovah or Christ Mind. Then the sense consciousness began to rule and the materialization of the body resulted.

Degeneration of the whole man followed. Loss of ability to draw constantly on the one and only source of life threw the whole race into an anemic condition. Their bodies began to disintegrate, and death came into the world. Then Satan, the mind of sense, began to rule; sin was in the saddle. The people like sheep had gone astray; they were lost in the wilderness of sense; they were in the throes of race extinction. New life had to be imparted; a blood transfusion was imperative. Christ then began a series of physical incarnations, beginning prehistorically and ending with His Jesus incarnation.

Why does the all-powerful God have to resort to the limitations of law to attain creative ends? We can only reply that there is no evidence anywhere in nature that any end has ever been accomplished except through the work of law. As men make civil laws and enforce them with penalties, even to death, so the human race has formed laws of physical birth and death, laws of sickness and physical inability, laws making food the source of bodily existence, laws of mind recognizing no other source of existence except the physical, the material.

The total of these race laws has formed a race consciousness separate from and independent of creative Mind, and when that Mind sought to help men spiritually, the mind of the flesh opposed it and made every effort to solve its problems in its own way.

The way of the flesh always proved futile and

disastrous because of human selfishness and greed.

Thus it became absolutely necessary for Christ, the Father of us all, to make closer contact with our physical or fleshly consciousness and pour into it a new life current. So Christ Himself, the Jehovah of the Old Testament, incarnated in Jesus and brought to our immediate attention both spiritually and physically the abundant life of primal being, Elohim God. Hence the proclamation of Christ in Jesus, "I came that they may have life, and may have *it* abundantly."

Modern scientists explain that the atoms that build molecules, cells, and tissues are composed of electrical units; that these units seem to contain the elements that convey life to all creation; that the cells of our body are energized by these life-giving atoms; and that the ether filling all space is heavily charged with this life-giving electricity. Science does not say that this omnipresent energy is divine life, nor does it admit that it is moved by mind, either divine or human. But spiritual discernment reveals that there is but one life and one intelligence penetrating and permeating man and the universe and that where there is evidence of life there is evidence of Being. Consequently the life-giving atom is the life-giving God, whom we conceive according to our degree of spiritual unfoldment.

If we have developed the mind of the Spirit, we see and feel the quickening life of the energy at the center of the atoms of our body. All spiritual concepts begin in the mind and are translated into atomic life in the body. Here we have the point of contact between the Christ life and the race life. It also explains why our life as a people was no longer receiving the energy flow from the parent stream. Like the prodigal son, we had gone into a country far from the Father, and there was a famine in that land. We were starving for the divine substance and got no satisfaction out of the husks, the food of the swine.

Because of the gulf between the Mind of Being and the sense mind of the race, no life flow was possible. Then Christ incarnate in the flesh through Jesus offered His body as a life or electrical transformer. The atomic units of His body were sundered and sown as points of life and light in our mind and body atmosphere, to the end that anyone who concentrates his thoughts on Christ in faith will attract as a spiritual magnet one or many of His body atoms. These Christ atoms, appropriated by the individual, become food and drink and form the nucleus of a regenerated body for the person appropriating them.

This casting forth of His life and body for the regeneration of His people is promised in the use of the bread and wine as symbols, in the Last Supper, as described in the 26th chapter of Matthew. "And as they were eating, Jesus took bread, and blessed, and brake it; and he gave to the disciples, and said, Take, eat; this is my body. And he took a cup, and gave thanks, and gave to them, saying, Drink ye all of it; for this is my blood of the covenant, which is poured out for many unto remission of sins."

Thus Jesus gave His life and body substance as a kind of blood transfusion to a dying race, and the agony in Gethsemane was the contemplation of the wrenching of the central ego of the trillions of living electrons, protons, atoms, molecules, and cells composing His organism. Thus the body and life elements of the Christ body were sown as seed in the soil of our race mind, and it is our privilege to appropriate and incorporate these precious elements into our mind and body.

The body of Christ Jesus is not to be subject to permanent disintegration and death; in the creative processes of God it must be made part of our redeemed body and restored to its parent source, the Christ. As He said, "Therefore doth the Father love me, because I lay down my life, that I may take it again."

Here also we have made clear the mystery of salvation through the blood of Christ. It is not a miracle nor a personal sacrifice, but a meeting of a crisis in the race evolution by the transfusion of life from a Father to His perishing children. Understanding this in the sense of its scientific reality should make us every one more energetic in taking advantage of our only means of escape from the ills of the flesh and insuring our ultimate salvation. "Pray that ye enter not into temptation" is translated by

Fenton, "Pray, for fear trial should overtake you." The same idea is brought out in the Lord's Prayer, which in the King James Version reads, "Lead us not into temptation," but which, according to good authorities should be, "You would not lead us into temptation, nor forsake us in trial." The petition is for strength to overcome trial.

As Paul so tellingly wrote to the Philippians: "Finally, brethren, whatsoever things are true, whatsoever things are honorable, whatsoever things are just, whatsoever things are pure, whatsoever things are lovely, whatsoever things are of good report; if there be any virtue, and if there be any praise, think on these things."

The Lenten Lessons

Lent

THE WORD LENT comes from the Anglo-Saxon word for spring, which is derived from a verb meaning to lengthen. Lent comes in the spring when the days become noticeably longer.

This annual season of fasting, prayer, and penitence has been observed by the Western Church since the first century after Christ, although it has not always been forty days long. In more recent times it has been kept forty days, after the example of Moses and Elijah, and to commemorate the forty days of fasting and prayer that Jesus spent in the wilderness.

The first day of Lent is called Ash Wednesday from the custom that prevailed in the early Church of sprinkling ashes on the heads of penitents on the first day of Lent, in token of repentance for sin.

Ash Wednesday comes forty-six days before Easter. There are six Sundays in Lent, and they are not considered part of Lent, because in the Western Church Sunday is always a feast day. The forty weekdays beginning with Ash Wednesday constitute Lent.

The fifth Sunday in Lent is known as Passion Sunday, because it marks the beginning of Passiontide, the last two weeks of Lent. These two weeks specifically commemorate the Passion of Jesus, or His experiences following the Last Supper.

The last week of Lent is called Holy Week. It includes Palm Sunday, Maundy Thursday, and Good Friday.

Palm Sunday, the Sunday before Easter, commemorates Jesus' entrance into Jerusalem when the people strewed palms in His way.

Maundy Thursday, the Thursday before Easter, is a corruption of the Latin word *mandati* meaning "of the commandment," and refers to the command "This do in remembrance of me" spoken by Jesus in regard to His breaking of the bread and drinking of the wine at the Last Supper. Maundy Thursday commemorates the event of the Last Supper.

Good Friday, the Friday before Easter, probably known originally as God's Friday, commemorates the crucifixion of Jesus.

Easter Day, of course, commemorates the Resurrection. The word *Easter* comes from the Anglo-Saxon word *Eastre,* the name of the Goddess of spring, in whose honor a festival was celebrated each April. Easter Day always comes on the first Sunday after the full moon that occurs on or after March 21. If the full moon falls on a Sunday, Easter is the next Sunday. Easter can never fall earlier than March 22 nor later than April 25.

* * *

Lent is a season of spiritual growth, a time for progressive unfoldment. When we can blend and merge our mind with God-Mind, the way is open for the Lord to glorify us and to lift us into a higher, purer, more spiritual state.

"Where two or three are gathered together in

my name, there am I in the midst of them," said Jesus. Unity students everywhere are invited to participate yearly in our Lenten program. Christ is in our midst, as the God of our planet, as the one great Teacher. Place all burdens on the Lord and enter the Lenten season expecting definite results.

Fasting means abstaining from; it is abstinence. The place of overcoming is in the consciousness of man. The forty-day fast is an all-round denial of sense demands. In fasting, we as metaphysicians abstain from error thinking and meditate on spiritual Truth until we incorporate it into the consciousness of oneness with the Father.

The desire to excel is in all men. It is the inspiration of the Holy Spirit, which ever urges us on through earth toward heaven. It should be encouraged and cultivated in the right direction.

As day after day we steadily adhere to our firm resolve to follow the steps outlined for the Lenten season, we discover that we are building on a firm foundation, and are mounting into a higher consciousness. We come to know that Christ is indeed with us and is resurrecting in us His realizations of light, life, and substance.

Denial

1st Day, Ash Wednesday. Read Matthew 5:1-16.

Ash Wednesday, the first day of Lent, is so-called from the ceremonial of ashes. Ashes symbolize repentance.

John the Baptist came, saying, "Repent ye; for the kingdom of heaven is at hand." Repentance means denial; it is a relinquishment and should be made without too much vehemence. Therefore, I deny out of consciousness old error thoughts, as if I were gently sweeping away cobwebs, and I affirm positively and fearlessly that I am a child of God, and that my inheritance is from Him.

As I follow this rule I find that I am letting go of old mortal beliefs and the Divine within is flaming higher and higher. Its pure white light is infusing all my surroundings with a delightful spirit of wisdom, dignity, and peace. I realize more and more the law of righteous thinking that is bringing me into a consciousness of my perfect dominion.

In Christ it is not difficult to eliminate belief in strife and contention. If petty quarrels, jealousy, uncharitable thoughts come into my life, I overcome them by a quiet but positive denial made in the realization that no error has any power or reality in itself. I turn away from the belief in negation, and my thinking changes. I rid my consciousness of limited thoughts that have encumbered and darkened my understanding. I break down mortal thought and ascend into a spiritual realm, the kingdom of the heavens.

In the spirit of divine love I affirm: *"Forgetting the things that are behind, I realize I am strong, positive, powerful, wise, loving, fearless, free spirit. I am God's perfect child."*

Affirmation

2d Day, Thursday. Read Luke 7:1-17.

The science of Spirit is the orderly study of truths formulated in Divine Mind according to the operation of universal law. An affirmation is a positive and orderly statement of Truth. By affirmation we claim and appropriate that which is ours.

The Word is the working power of Divine Mind. One will never go down to defeat if in his hour of need he positively affirms the almightiness of God-Mind through Christ, and invokes its help in his behalf.

I declare that as a child of God I am now entering the Christ consciousness of perfection. This is in itself an affirmation, the highest I can make. Jesus helped Himself into this high state of being by His use of the spoken word. He continually made the very highest affirmations such as, "I and the Father are one," "All authority hath been given unto me in heaven and on earth." I am joint heir with Jesus to the infinite good of the kingdom, and by the faithful use of my spoken word I claim my heavenly good.

Faith is the result of many affirmations. Each affirmation helps to build up a substantial, firm, unwavering state of mind, because it establishes Truth in consciousness.

As day by day I repeat and courageously live affirmations of Truth, I come to know that I am opening a channel of intelligent communication with the silent forces at the depths of being; thoughts and words therefrom flow forth, and I realize an entirely new source of power developing within me.

I affirm: *"Through Jesus Christ I realize my divine sonship, and I am transformed into His image and likeness."*

God

3d Day, Friday. Read John 15:1-16.

"God is Spirit: and they that worship him must worship in spirit and truth." We do not see God with our physical eyes excepting as He manifests Himself through His works. His attributes are therefore brought into expression by man who is His son and who is like Him in essence. Jesus was a true expression of God because He was like Him. If we would manifest the divine attributes, we must seek to attain the consciousness and the understanding that characterized Jesus. We must endeavor to raise our thoughts and feelings to God's level if we would make ourselves channels through which

He can come forth into expression and manifestation.

God transcendent suggests God as above and beyond His creation. This idea of God as remote from the practical affairs of man or from man's own experience is false. God (perfection) is not out of reach of His offspring nor something beyond or above them. Tennyson tells us that "closer is He than breathing, and nearer than hands and feet."

I am centered in God because I focus my attention on His ideas and ideals. The Holy Spirit, which is the Word of God in action, leads me into a consciousness of my divine sonship and inheritance. My inheritance from Him is executive ability, abundant supply, faithfulness, joy, all good. "I am thy portion and thine inheritance."

In the name of Jesus Christ I declare: *"God's perfect plan of bodily perfection is bearing fruit, and I am made whole."*

I AM

4th Day, Saturday. Read John 10:1-18.

I am a child of the Father, and my inheritance is from Him. I AM is the Christ within me, the true spiritual being, whom God made in His image and likeness. Through the I AM (the Christ), I link myself with the Father, with Spirit, with life, wisdom, love, peace, strength, power, and Truth.

I AM is the gate through which my thoughts

come forth from the invisible, and it is through this gate that I go to get into the presence of Spirit.

The I AM has its being in heaven; its home is in the realm of God ideals. I hitch my I AM to the star of God, and infinite joy follows as night the day.

The I AM always assures me that the preponderance of power is in spiritual things. Fear throws dust in one's eyes and hides the mighty spiritual forces that are always with one. I deny ignorance and fear, and affirm the presence and power of the I AM. "I AM THAT I AM . . . I AM hath sent me unto you."

I realize that spiritual character is the rock foundation of being. As I build my consciousness in God-Mind, I find that I am in heaven right here on earth. I let go of the little self and take hold of the big self. "Not my will, but thine, be done." The I AM is the will in its highest aspect. The will may be said to be the man, because it is the directive power that decides the character formation which makes what is called individuality.

I boldly affirm: *"I am a child of God, and I am joint heir with Jesus to abiding life, wisdom, love, peace, substance, strength, and power."*

The Altar

1st Sunday. Read Matthew 5:21-26.

The altar represents a fixed, definite center in the consciousness of man. It is a place within where we meet the Lord face to face and are willing to give up our sins, give up the lower for the higher, the personal for the impersonal, the animal for the divine.

The altar, mentioned in Revelation 11:1 symbolizes the consciousness of full consecration that takes place in the temple of worship, the body. "Present your bodies a living sacrifice, holy, acceptable to God, *which is* your spiritual service."

The altar to the unknown God is a yearning to know the unrevealed Spirit, and a reaching out of the mind for a fuller realization of its source.

Prayer does not change God—it changes us. Sincere desire is a form of prayer. Deep desire is essential for spiritual growth. It is desire—earnest, intense desire—that draws the whole being up out of mortality and its transient joys into the power to appreciate and receive real spiritual blessings. This is a demonstration, the proving of a Truth principle in one's body and affairs. It is the manifestation of an ideal when its accomplishment has been brought about by one's conformity in thought, word, and act, to the creative principle of God.

Kneeling at the altar I take my statement of Truth and hold it steadily in mind until I get my realization, the logic of my mind is satisfied, and there is the lifting up and expanding of soul consciousness.

To this end I affirm: *"It is not I, 'but the Father abiding in me doeth his works.' "*

The Garden of Eden

5th Day, Monday. Read John 14:1-12.

Man's body temple is the outer expression of the Garden of Eden, which God gave him to keep and to trim. Man's primary work in the earthly consciousness (the Garden) is to use his creative power to preserve harmony and order in his world, and to conserve his powers for divine direction.

The Garden of Eden represents a region of being within, in which are provided all primal ideas for the production of the beautiful. It represents the elemental life and intelligence placed at the disposal of man, through which he is to evolve a spiritual mind and a spiritual body.

The Garden is the spiritual body in which man dwells when he brings forth thoughts after the pattern of the original divine ideas. The Garden is the substance of God.

God's greatest gift to man is the power of thought, through which he can incorporate into his consciousness the Mind of God.

There are twelve gates which open into this wonderful Garden of Eden. These gates are the twelve faculties of mind: faith, strength, wisdom, love, power, imagination, understanding, will, law or order, zeal, renunciation, life. Each faculty, through the most accelerated mind action, as in prayer, has been purified and therefore opens into the very heart of the Holy City within.

I affirm: *"My body is the temple of God, cleansed, purified, undefiled, made perfect. Praise God!"*

Faith

6th Day, Tuesday. Read Hebrews 11:1-12.

Faith is the perceiving power of the mind linked with a power to shape substance. It is spiritual assurance, the power to do the seemingly impossible. It is a force that draws to us our heart's desire right out of the invisible spiritual substance. It is a deep inner knowing that that which is sought is already ours for the taking, the "assurance of *things* hoped for."

Faith working in spiritual substance accomplishes all things. This is the faith that co-operates with creative law. Exercised in spiritual consciousness, it finds its abode, and without variation or disappointment it brings results that are seemingly miraculous.

Faith in the reality of things spiritual develops the faith center in man's brain. When the mental eye is illumined with faith, it sheds a radiance that hovers like a halo around the head and extends in lessening degree throughout the whole body. "When thine eye is single, thy whole body also is full of light."

The halo that the early artists painted around the heads of the saints was not imaginary, but real. This illuminating power of faith covers the whole constitution of man, making him master of all the forces centering about spiritual consciousness.

I realize that my faith in the invisible is building a real abiding substance in my mind and in my body. Spiritual ideas grow quickly when planted in the rich soil of my mind, and my body temple changes accordingly.

I affirm: *"I have faith in the glorious infusion of the more abundant life of Christ vitalizing me. I am lifted up and healed."*

Strength

7th Day, Wednesday. Read Matthew 4:1-11.

Strength is freedom from weakness; stability of character, power to withstand temptation. It is the force or power to do, capacity to accomplish. "The name of Jehovah is a strong tower; the righteous runneth into it, and is safe." Strength originates in Spirit; the thought and the word spiritually expressed bring the manifestation.

Jesus is the greatest teacher. He is the type that I am striving to follow, not only in spiritual culture and in mind culture, but in body culture. By faithfully studying and using the methods of Jesus I am bringing forth the very best that is in me.

Through Christ the mind and the body of man have the power of using strength on various planes of consciousness. I affirm that I am steadfast and strong in thought and in deed, and thus I am establishing strength in soul and in body. I refuse to let the thought of weakness enter my consciousness, but always ignore the suggestion and affirm myself to be a tower of strength within and without.

Supreme strength as demonstrated by Jesus can be attained by one who trusts in Spirit and conserves his vital substance. The strength of Spirit is necessary to the perpetuation of soul and body and to the overcoming of death.

As I relax more and more and lift my consciousness to harmonize with the ever-present perfect Mind, I am invigorated and restored to stabilizing power. No harm can befall me. I am made strong through Spirit.

I affirm: *"The joy of the Lord is a wellspring within me, and I am established in divine strength."*

Wisdom

8th Day, Thursday. Read Matthew 7:1-12.

Wisdom is of Spirit. One can get flashes of understanding at any time, but the clear light of the Supreme shines steadily on us as we become obedient and receptive to the Supreme's monitions. Jesus always listened for the "inner voice," and was obedient to it in His meek and lowly work among the humblest class of men.

Spiritual discernment always places wisdom above the other faculties of mind. It is pure knowing, and comes by kindling the inner light. "The wisdom that is from above is first pure, then peaceable."

This means that as I call the righteous judge into action I may find my standards of right and wrong undergoing rapid changes, but if I hold steadily to the Lord as my supreme guide, I shall be led into all righteousness.

As I dwell upon this all-knowing faculty within, I become conscious of the Christ radiance lighting my mind, and my whole being is illumined. My thoughts are quickened through their conscious relationship to Spirit. I am flooded with new life, which raises my organism above the disintegrating thought currents of the earth; and thus I am not only redeeming my mind, but am also saving the flesh from corruption.

Spiritual understanding reveals that the resurrection of the body from death is not to be confined to Jesus, but is for all men who comprehend Truth and apply it as Jesus applied it.

Realizing that I am awakening to the reality of my higher self, I affirm: *"Christ within me is my glory. The brightness of His presence wipes out all darkness, and I am filled with life and light."*

Love

9th Day, Friday. Read I John 4:7-21.

Love, in Divine Mind, is the idea of universal unity. In expression, it is the power that joins and binds together the universe and everything in it. Love is a harmonizing, constructive power. When it is made active in consciousness, it conserves substance and reconstructs, rebuilds, and restores man and his world.

As I make a perfect union between my mind and the loving mind of the Father, I realize a goodness everlasting and joy beyond expression. The point of contact is a willingness and a seeking on my part. "Seek, and ye shall find; knock, and it shall be opened unto you."

Love is that mighty power, that divine quality of God that is expressing through all mankind, and cannot be suppressed by any outside force. I now firmly declare that it is expressing through me, and that no environment or external condition can hinder it. Any unloving condition of the world is no bar to my exercise of love; in fact, it is an incentive.

I am not afraid to pour out my love on all the so-called evil of the world. I deny the appearance of evil, and affirm the omnipotence of love and goodness.

The word *love* overcomes hate, resistance, opposition, obstinacy, anger, jealousy, and all other error states where there is mental or physical friction. As divine love enters into the thought process, every cell of my body is poised and balanced in space, in right mathematical order as to weight and relative distance.

In quietness and confidence, I affirm: *"God, in His love, fills me with new life. In His name I am cleansed, strengthened, and healed."*

Power

10th Day, Saturday. Read Luke 4:31-44.

Man controls his thoughts and his feelings by the use of his innate power. A quickening from on high must precede his realization of dominion. "Ye shall receive power, when the Holy Spirit is come upon you."

Man is the power of God in action. The power to control his thinking is the highest gift given to man. There is a universal, creative force that urges man forward to the recognition of the creative power of individual thought.

The word *Jehovah* (Christ) is charged with spiritual power far above and beyond any other word in human language.

The power center in the throat is the open door between the formless and the formed worlds of vibration pertaining to the expression of sound. When the voice has united with the life of the soul, it takes on a sweetness and a depth that one feels and remembers. But sweeter and deeper still is the voice of one who has made union with Spirit and can say with Jesus, "Heaven and earth shall pass away, but my words shall not pass away."

I cultivate a loving attitude of mind toward everybody, and my voice is rich, warm, and mellow. As I pray and realize spiritual dominion, I feel vital and energetic and my voice is strong and vibrant and brilliant. Through these vibrations I feel the power of unity with the higher self more quickly than in any other way. "All power is given unto me in heaven [mind] and in earth [body]."

In His name I affirm: *"All the issues of my life are stirred to action by the quickening Christ power, and I have dominion over my thoughts and my feelings."*

Imagination

2d Sunday. Read Acts 10:9-35.

The imagination is that faculty of mind which images and forms. Everything that is manifest was first a mental picture and was brought into expression by this forming power. Man accumulates a mass of ideas about substance and life, and with his imagination he molds them into shape.

Those who look to the Holy Spirit for guidance find that its instruction is given to all who believe in Christ, and the command is to make all things after the pattern shown Moses on the Mount as found in Exodus 25:40.

The Spirit of truth projects into the chamber of imagery pictures that, rightly understood, will be a sure guide for all people who believe in the omnipresence of mind. The imagination will carry out any idea or set of ideas that the I AM reflects into it, hence theories are not to be trusted. There must be evidence in works. This is accomplished by the working power of the world.

With my imagination I lay hold of perfect ideas and clothe them with substance. My body is the product of my mind. In my communication with God, the imagining power of my mind is playing an important part. It receives divine ideas, and in dreams and visions reflects their character in the consciousness. According to the Scriptures this is the opening of the heavens and the seeing the "angels of God ascending and descending upon the Son of man."

With my imagination fixed on Spirit, I affirm: *"In the quietness and confidence of Spirit, I see myself as God sees me, His perfect image and likeness."*

Understanding

11th Day, Monday. Read Luke 2:40:52.

Spiritual understanding is the ability of the mind to apprehend and realize the laws of thought and the relation of ideas one to another. It is that something through which we understand God and ourselves.

Understanding reveals that love and wisdom should work together, that power should be expressed through love, and zeal should be tempered with wisdom.

Intellectual understanding comes first in the soul's development, then a deeper understanding of Principle follows, until the whole man ripens into wisdom.

Those who are being educated in Truth through the power of the word will finally arrive at the place where the true light from Spirit will dawn on them, and they will see with spiritual understanding and have proof of the reality of the Christ Mind.

I realize that God is supreme knowing. That in me which comprehends is understanding; it knows and compares in wisdom. Its comparisons are not made in the realm of form, but in the realm of ideas. Understanding is that in me which knows how to accomplish things. I claim my Christ understanding at all times.

If willfulness of the mortal tries to take over, I gently deny it power, and affirm for spiritual understanding. At all times I hold for absolute freedom in the Lord. God is the one principle; we are all as free to use God as we are free to use the principle of mathematics or music. The principle never interferes, but if it is to be rightly applied, I must develop understanding.

I affirm: *"Divine understanding in me unites with the Holy Spirit, and I always know what to do."*

Will

12th Day, Tuesday. Read John 1:1-18.

The will is the executive power of the mind. The commandments of Jesus teach the Father's will. Those who keep them are therefore at one with the will of God.

It is possible to get very close to the kingdom of heaven by doing good works and surrendering to Spirit the various faculties of the mind, but we can never fully enter into and abide in heaven, or divine harmony, without surrendering all that makes up the personality, of which the will is the center.

The will may be said to be the man, because it is the directive power that determines character formation. When man wills the will of God to be done, he forms spiritual character. The use of the regenerate will is for the sole purpose of spiritual unfoldment.

When the will of man adheres to wisdom faithfully, and carries out in its work the plans that are idealized in wisdom, it creates in man a consciousness of harmony and peace. Spirit breathes into such an individual continually the necessary inspiration and knowledge to give him superior understanding.

I bring the divine will to bear in my consciousness by understanding, by appropriating universal wisdom, by affirming, "Not my will, but thine, be done." God is potential, unformed will; man is manifest God will. I now link my will with the principle of divine force in order to develop superior executive capacity. After this manner I am swiftly bringing forth faculties that under the slow action of mortality would take ages to develop.

I affirm: *"The will of God is uppermost in my consciousness, and I am glorified in my understanding."*

Law

13th Day, Wednesday. Read Galatians 6:1-10, 16.

Divine law is the logical process by which divine principle, or God, manifests. The inner spirit of the law is the spiritual way of life that Jesus taught and lived.

Divine law is the universal something in us of which we all are conscious, and tells us when we are doing right and when we are doing wrong. It may be defined as the innate knowing of right and wrong, and this knowing may be quickened. The quickening does not come by the study of material things, but by concentrating the mind on the Christ. Man does not make the law; the law is, and it was established for our benefit before the world was formed.

There is a law of spiritual and mental growth constantly at work in the mind, raising man from sense consciousness to spiritual consciousness. The nature of the universe is purity and goodness. Abiding in the Christ consciousness, man aligns himself with divine law. He becomes "the light of the world."

Today I find I am one with the infinite law of expansion—one with the principle of never-ceasing growth and development toward the fulfillment of God's perfect idea that is firmly infixed in all creation.

Divine law cannot be broken. It holds man responsible for the result of his labors. "The law of the Spirit of life in Christ Jesus" is the action of true ideas working in my mind and in my body.

I affirm: *"My house is set in order, and I press forward toward the goal of perfection."*

Zeal

14th Day, Thursday. Read Luke 10:30-42; 11:1-4.

Zeal is the affirmative impulse of existence; its command is, "Go forward!" Zeal is the mighty force that incites all things to action; the eternal urge behind all things. To be without zeal is to be without the zest of living. Zeal and enthusiasm incite to glorious achievement in every ideal that the mind conceives.

Zeal should be tempered with wisdom. Some persons get so fired with zeal when they first tackle a job, that they quickly grow tired, and fail to carry it through to completion. The need is for control, equalization.

Watch the pull of a giant locomotive; note how it slowly but steadily moves forward, almost by inches at first but gradually increasing until its mile-long train swiftly disappears in the distance.

"The zeal of thy house hath eaten me up" means that the zeal faculty has become so active intellectually that it has consumed the vitality and left nothing for spiritual growth. Excessive zeal in religious forms of worship eats up the purely spiritual. When we become very zealous in observing the rites of the church we are prone to forget the church itself, which is Christ.

The divine command is, "Take time to be holy." I am quick to do the bidding of Spirit and use a portion of my zeal in establishing God's kingdom within me. I do not put all my enthusiasm into helping others; my own unfoldment is of great importance to me. I love to aid my brother, but I do not allow that idea to rob me of the power to demonstrate Truth for myself.

I affirm: *"My zeal is tempered with wisdom, and I maintain a perfect balance within and without."*

Renunciation

15th Day, Friday. Read Matthew 18:21-35.

The accumulated effects of sins of past lives, is a burden that those who accept it expect to carry for ages, or until they work out of it. They are weary treadmill travelers from birth to death. There is no such hopeless note in the doctrine of Jesus. He came to bring a full consciousness of abundant life, complete forgiveness, redemption from all sin, and victory over death and the grave.

The law is Truth, and the truth is that all is good. There is no power and no reality in sin. If sin were real and enduring, like goodness and Truth, it could not be forgiven but would hold its victim forever. As I enter into the understanding of the real and the unreal, a great light dawns on me, and

I see what Jesus meant when He said, "The Son of man hath authority on earth to forgive sins."

The Son of man is that in me which discerns the difference between Truth and error. As I get this understanding, I am in position to free my soul from sin and my body from disease, which is the effect of sin. In spiritual understanding the I AM of man forgives or "gives" Truth "for" error; the mind is set in order, and the body healed. The moment man realizes this he puts himself in harmony with the Truth of Being, and the law wipes out all his transgressions.

In His name I affirm: *"The law of the Spirit of life in Christ Jesus makes me free from the law of sin and of death."*

Life

16th Day, Saturday. Read John 4:1-26.

Life is a phase of Being, the expression of which manifests as animation, activity, and vigor. The consciousness of eternal life places one in the stream of life that never fails.

The whole race needs a spiritual quickening of the life principle; its origin is in Divine Mind. Life is the gift of God. "Stir up the gift of God, which is in thee." To think intently about life is to quicken it into action. To talk about energy, force, power, life, will make the life currents flow swiftly throughout the whole being.

To Jesus the God presence was an abiding flame

—a flame of life everlasting that He felt in every cell of His body making Him more and more alive, cleansing and purifying Him until He became every whit perfect.

By mastering carnality Jesus opened the way for all men to attain eternal life. During our higher realizations of Truth we are often conscious of this abiding flame working in and through us.

I now make alive all the cells in my organism by mentally infusing into them the Christ consciousness. This is the new birth, which is transforming my body and raising it to electrical energy. This was carried to its fulfillment by Jesus in the resurrection of His body. The next step in divine evolution is the spiritualization of the body, or the Ascension.

The quickening life in me is now brought into expression by my holding and repeating this statement of Truth:

"I have the Mind of Christ. My words are spiritually quickened and they are alive forevermore. I am filled with the vitality and vigor and health of Jesus Christ."

Conservation

3d Sunday. Read Isaiah 55:1-13.

We should ever remember that our youth, which we love so well, never really dies; it merely falls asleep in the realm of the subconscious. People grow old because they let the youth idea fall asleep. By using spiritual understanding they can awaken it.

The awakening of youthful energies is necessary to one in the regeneration. The body cannot be refined and made, like its Creator, eternal before all the thoughts necessary to its perpetuation are revived in it.

Jesus represents man in the regeneration; that is, man in the process of restoring his body to its pristine purity where it will live on perpetually without old age, disease, or death. A necessary step in this process of body restoration is the quickening of the vitalizing energies in the subconsciousness that feed the body and give it the life force that renews its youth. Eternal youth is one of the God-given ideas that man loves.

Waste of substance is the great sin that results in body disintegration. It is the sense mind that causes all waste, whether in the organism or in the more external realm called the world. Jesus came to save men from sin and to make them ready for an abundant entrance into the glorious kingdom of Christ, which is to be established on the earth.

We can get at the subject of conservation definitely by considering the life "hid with Christ in God," for the hidden protected life is the conserved life.

I now make conscious union with the substance of all spiritual attributes as I affirm:

"Through Christ the divine economy is active in me, and I conserve the spiritual essences in all phases of my life."

Jesus Christ Our Helper

17th Day, Monday. Read Romans 8:1-11.

If God had not planned to make Jesus a continuous working factor in our civilization there would be no good purpose for His having been sent, and for the great sacrifice that He made. He came to show us "the way, and the truth, and the life," and He promised "Lo, I am with you always." He also promised that He would be with us as a teacher. "When he, the Spirit of truth, is come, he shall guide you into all the truth."

No one is overlooked. The helpful hand of Jesus is extended to all. Whoever you are, wherever you are, Jesus in His spiritual consciousness is waiting for your mental recognition. Whatever your object, He will show you how to attain it. "Whatsoever ye shall ask in my name, that will I do."

Jesus developed the innate powers of mind and body and thereby became a citizen of the heavens or realms where dwell the sons of God. He did this by the power of His word—by releasing the imprisoned electrons of His body and raising them to spiritual consciousness.

Why do we not see Jesus? Optics show that man's eyes are limited in sight. They are aware of rays of light within a very narrow range. The microscope reveals a world of living things to which the natural eye is utterly oblivious. Both below and above the range of human vision living entities exist. We sometimes feel the presence of what we cannot see.

Affirm: *"I rejoice in the restorative power of Jesus Christ now working mightily in a new consciousness of life in my soul and body."*

Evolution

18th Day, Tuesday. Read Romans 8:18-39.

In every man the Christ, or the Word of God, is infolded; it is an idea that contains ideas.

Evolution is the result of the development of ideas in mind. What we are is the result of the evolution of our consciousness, and our consciousness is the result of the seed ideas sown in our mind. Therefore spiritual evolution is the unfolding of the Spirit of God into expression. It is the development achieved by man working under spiritual law. Humanity is the garden of God, of which the soil is the omnipresent thought substance.

The Christ, or Word (Son) of God evolution of man is plainly taught in the New Testament as the supreme attainment of every man. "For the earnest expectation of the creation waiteth for the revealing of the sons of God."

Without some evidence in us of the Christ man we are little better than animals. When through faith in the reality of things spiritual we begin soul evolution there is great rejoicing; "we rejoice in hope of the glory of God."

Christianity teaches the complete law of evolution. "God said," and thus God created that which was to appear, God planned man and the universe, and through His word projected them into creation as ideal principles and immanent energies acting behind and within all visibility.

I affirm: *"I am one with the ever unfolding, ever increasing Spirit of divine understanding. My whole consciousness is ripening into perfection."*

The Blood of Jesus

19th Day, Wednesday. Read John 6:41-65.

Through the power of His word Jesus purified and spiritualized the natural blood in His body until it became a spiritual life stream, into which all may enter and be cleansed.

Through the power of His word Jesus broadcast the spiritual electrons of His body into the race thought atmosphere, that they may be apprehended by all who believe in Him.

This Lenten season I realize that I am baptized in His spiritual life stream, and am purified and cleansed. The electrons of His blood, which I appropriate, are centers of energy and life within, and they uplift and strengthen me.

Jesus called the bread He had blessed His body and the wine His blood. As I appropriate words of Truth, "eat them" so to speak, I partake of the substance and life of Spirit and build the Christ body. Thus I partake of the body and blood of Jesus, the true sacrament that vitalizes the body by renewing the mind.

The blood of Jesus in me is the life contained in God. The crown of life is attained by living eternally in the presence of God. Attainment depends on the understanding of the science of right thinking. My way to eternal life lies in my acknowledgment of my oneness with the Christ of God.

In His name I am gradually transforming and regenerating my blood and my body. Thus I am saved by Jesus Christ.

Realizing victory over every limited belief of the mortal, I affirm: *"I rejoice in the restorative power of Jesus' blood now working mightily in me to renew, to restore, and to make every whit whole."*

The Body Temple

20th Day, Thursday. Read Matthew 6:16-34.

God created the idea of the body as a self-perpetuating, self-renewing organism, which man reconstructs into his personal body. God created the body idea, and man, by his thinking manifests.

I realize that I shall have a perfect body and a perfect world when I understand and use the perfect word, the word that contains all the attributes of God. Therefore, I declare that my words are being charged with a full understanding of Divine Mind and its inhering ideas, and that I consciously apply this understanding in all of my feeling, thinking, speaking, and living and am therefore steadily putting on the Christ in mind and body.

Overcoming step by step the limitations of material thought, my body becomes more refined and increasingly radiant.

The law is that my body is transformed by the renewing of the mind. By affirmation the mind lays hold of living words of Truth and builds them into the body. As I enter into and abide in the Son of God consciousness I have eternal life and my body is transformed into pure flesh manifesting the perfection of Spirit.

To bless is to invoke good on that which is blessed. It is to confer God's good on something or someone. Therefore I bless my body temple, and declare its purity and strength and beauty. I pour out upon my body temple the oil of love and clothe it in garments of praise.

Realizing that the body of Christ in me is the result of my spiritual thought that maintains its unity with Spirit even in manifestation, I affirm:

"The Word of God in me quickens my mind. and my body is transformed into the likeness of His glorious body."

The Grace of God

21st Day, Friday. Read Matthew 5:17-20, 38-48.

"As far as the east is from the west,
So far hath he removed our transgressions from us."

Grace means good will, favor, disposition to

show mercy. Therefore, we do not hold ourselves as bond servants of the law, but as recipients of the grace of God, as sons of the Most High.

The grace of God extends to all people, not alone to one sect or creed. All men are equal in favor with God.

The grace of God is greater than the laws of man. We may make certain laws and restrictions for ourselves and "his servants ye are whom ye obey." If we are servants of the law, our obedience is unto death; if we are servants of righteousness, our obedience is unto life. To become recipients of that which the Father would bestow, we should take the element of grace into consideration; that even beyond what we ask, seek, earn, or deserve under the law, God is more than willing to give.

God, as the great creative principle of the universe, will always meet us more than half way. By becoming receptive to the "grace of God," we receive the measure of God's provision, which exceeds any of our imaginings.

I realize that "grace and truth came through Jesus Christ"; that is, the real saving, redeeming, transforming power comes to me through the work that Jesus did in establishing for the race a new and higher consciousness in the earth. I enter into that consciousness by faith in Him and by means of the inner spirit of the law that He taught and practiced.

I affirm: *"Through the grace of God I am forgiven and healed."*

Fourth Dimension

22d Day, Saturday. Read John 21:1-17.

The fourth dimension is that which embraces and encompasses the other three; it is realization, the doing away with time and space and all conditions. It is the process in which forms lose their apartness and become one under divine law. The human mind, with its limited reasoning faculties, is bound by time, space, and conditions. By itself it can get no further into the spiritual realm than reason will take it; but when we invoke the aid of the Christ in us we go beyond reason into the realm of pure realization; then we have attained the consciousness of pure be-ing, the fourth dimension of the being.

The one way to enter the realm of the fourth dimension, or of realization, is through scientific prayer, commonly named "the silence." First, I take with me the word *Jehovah* and go within and hold it steadily in mind, until the word illumines the whole inner consciousness. I am now functioning in the fourth dimension, and the way is open for concentrating on the prayer I have in mind for the special demonstration.

I fix my attention powerfully on the consummation of an idea until the idea has nucleated a certain amount of thought substance, and I am assured that it will be followed by that silent power of thought which, working throughout my whole being, is bringing forth the thing desired.

When my thoughts radiate with the speed of spiritual light, they blend with creative Mind (called by Jesus "heaven"), and that which I ask for is done.

I affirm: *"The illuminating power of Truth awakens and quickens my consciousness, and I discern clearly."*

The Sabbath

4th Sunday. Read Mark 2:23-28; 3:1-6.

The true Sabbath is the consciousness that we have fulfilled the divine law in both thought and act.

The sabbath is a very certain, definite thing. It is a state of mind that man enters or acquires when he goes into the silence, into the realm of Spirit. There he finds true rest and peace. The seventh day means the seventh or perfect stage of one's spiritual unfoldment. Man had become so lost in the darkness of sense consciousness that he could not save himself, so the Saviour came. When man lays hold of the indwelling Christ, the Saviour, he is raised out of the Adam consciousness into the Christ consciousness. He then enters the seventh stage of his unfoldment, where he finds sweet rest and peace.

The Sabbath as an institution was established by man. God does not rest from His work every seventh day, and there is no evidence that there has ever been a moment's cessation in the activity of the universe.

We do not quarrel with our brother over the observance of the Sabbath. If he says we should worship God on the seventh day, or on the first day, in either case we acquiesce. Not only do we do God's service in praise, song, and thanksgiving on the seventh day and the first day, but every day. In the true Sabbath our mind is turned to God every moment, and we are ever ready to acknowledge His holy presence in our heart and life. "The sabbath was made for man, and not man for the sabbath."

I affirm: *"I rest in the consciousness of the true Sabbath, and my heart is filled with joy and satisfaction."*

The Idea

23d Day, Monday. Read Luke 5:1-11.

In the Scriptures ideas are symbolized by fish. An idea is the original, primary, or unlimited thought of Being: in God-Mind, the eternal Word or Logos. In the idea are involved all the potentialities of that which is to be evolved through man. The idea itself becomes the evolving power through which it makes itself manifest.

Ideas are catching. We are all heavily charged with ideas. When ideas are released they spring forth and pass from mind to mind, being "recorded" as they fly; when they are expressed the whole race is lifted up—because true ideas are charged with the uplifting Spirit. We bring divine ideas into manifestation by making ourselves one with them, becoming conscious of our indwelling Christ Mind and our oneness with the Father.

As the son is to the father, so is the idea to the mind. Mind is one with its ideas, so the Father—God-Mind—is one with its offspring, the idea—the Son. Mind is coexistent with its ideas, and there is continual interaction and communion. The Father and the Son are one—are coexisting, interacting, and intercommuning in will and purpose. It was from the grand idea of divine life that Jesus healed the sick and raised the dead.

Spiritual inspiration in me is an inflow of divine ideas; activity of a spiritual character; understanding that comes from God. It is the inbreathing of Spirit. The breath of God infused into me has endowed me with super-life. "He breathed on them, and saith unto them, Receive ye the Holy Spirit."

I affirm: *"In the presence and power of the Christ idea in me, I proclaim my perfection."*

Healing

24th Day, Tuesday. Read Matthew 9:14-38.

Health, real health, is from within and does not have to be manufactured in the without. It is the normal condition of man, a condition true to the reality of his being.

The first step in all spiritual healing is the using of faith, and the next step is to become open and receptive to the stream of healing life. Spiritual healing restores to perpetual health because it erases the error thought and cleanses the mind.

Through the exercise of faith and our word, our spiritual quality is fused into unity with the power of Christ, and the healing is marvelously accomplished.

It is said that the early Christians, before going forth to do their mighty works, commanded the new life in Christ to come forth and to imbue their consciousness with its healing potency to such an extent that it would flow through them and heal all those to whom they ministered.

They discovered that when they repeated over and over the most powerful prayer Jesus ever uttered, the Lord's Prayer, the hidden Christ within each one of them was called into action. They further discovered that the fifteenth time they realized the prayer the waters of tribulation as well as all manner of diseases began to subside, and that their realization lifted the consciousness of those who were asking their help. All tribulation and disease dropped away.

Experience proves the power of words to bring health. In healing myself, I talk to my body, repeating necessary denials and affirmations. This raises my consciousness to spiritual reality where all healing power originates.

I faithfully affirm: *"Through Jesus Christ, God's vitalizing energy floods my whole being, and I am healed."*

Peace

25th Day, Wednesday. Read Matthew 5:14-40.

"Still in thy right hand carry gentle peace,
To silence envious tongues. Be just, and fear not:
Let all the ends thou aim'st at be thy country's
Thy God's and truth's."

—*Shakespeare*

The great thought waves that move the world are set into action by deep thinkers.

Peace and understanding of spiritual realities arise in the mind when it has made the inner contact. When we know the work of Spirit in transforming mind and body, we shall see that the crushing of personal ambitions releases spiritual ideas of far-reaching influence.

Jesus went back to the very source of all discord, and showed how all resistance and antagonism must cease. He did not stop to argue whether the cause was just or not, but He said, "Agree with thine adversary quickly"; "If any man would go to law with thee, and take away thy coat, let him have thy cloak also." To the mortal mind this seems like foolishness, but Jesus spoke out of the inner wisdom that knows that it is dangerous to allow any kind of opposing thoughts to form in consciousness. He knew that the universal law of justice would adjust all matters, if men would trust it and cease fighting mentally for their rights. This is accomplished by bringing the Christ, the Prince of Peace, to bear in all our affairs. "My peace I give unto you."

I praise God for the peace of my own higher self. I rejoice and am glad in the possession of the Holy City within. With my inner vision I see the gates open wide, and holy peace pervades my consciousness.

I affirm: *"My mind is stayed on Thee, and I rest in Thy peace and power."*

Heaven

26th Day, Thursday. Read Matthew 13:24-53.

God idealized two universal planes of consciousness, the heaven and the earth, or more properly, "the heavens and the earth." One is the realm of pure ideals; the other, of thought forms. God does not create the visible universe directly, as man makes cement pavement, but He creates the ideas that are used by His intelligent "image" and "likeness" to make the universe. Thus God's creations are always spiritual. Man's creations are both material and spiritual, according to his understanding.

Jesus, of all those claiming intimate acquaintance with spiritual things, gave heaven definite location. "The kingdom of God is within you." This kingdom is now ready. "The fields . . . are white already unto harvest." The conditions are ripe. But only those come in who are willing to exchange for it their ideas of earthly possessions. Every earthly link must be broken, every mortal love crucified. This is the way Jesus entered this kingdom, and His way is the way we must all employ.

Heaven is everywhere present. It is the orderly, lawful adjustment of God's kingdom in man's mind, body, and affairs; it is the Christ consciousness, the realm of divine ideas, a state of consciousness in harmony with the thoughts of God. Heaven is within every one of us; a place, a conscious sphere of mind, having all the attractions described or imagined as belonging to heaven.

I realize that faith in Spirit and the ultimate dominance of the good in me will restore me to the heavenly consciousness from which I descended.

I affirm: *"Heaven within is one perfect harmonious life, substance, and intelligence, and I rejoice."*

Principle

27th Day, Friday. Read John 5:19-47.

Principle and Truth are one. Divine Principle is Truth in a universal sense, or as it pertains to Elohim God. Satisfaction comes to us as we live according to Principle.

Universal Principle, the oversoul of this planet, was working its way into expression through Jesus. The same work that Jesus accomplished is being accomplished by all men—though perhaps very slowly.

To demonstrate Principle keep establishing yourself in certain statements (affirmations) of the law.

The more often you present to your mind a logical and true proposition, the stronger become the inner feeling of realization.

As the principle of music moves through tones, so does the principle of mind move through ideas. Therefore God, as Principle, moves through the expressed thought of Divine Mind.

The mind of each individual may be consciously unified with Divine Mind through the indwelling Christ. By affirming at-one-ment with God-Mind, we eventually realize the perfect mind which was in Christ Jesus.

"Have this mind in you, which was also in Christ Jesus: who, existing in the form of God, counted not the being on an equality with God a thing to be grasped, but emptied himself, taking the form of a servant, being made in the likeness of men."

I affirm: *"Principle is Truth. I know the Truth, and the Truth makes me free."*

Miracles

28th Day, Saturday. Read Matthew 14:15-36.

The first miracle in our consciousness is the transforming of the water of thought into the wine of thought, through introducing into the consciousness some of the "angels of God," or true ideas.

In reality miracles are events that take place as a result of the application of a higher law to certain conditions.

God never performs miracles, if by miracle is meant a departure from universal law. Whatever the prophets did was done by the operation of laws inherent in Being and open to the discovery of every man.

By the power of his thought Elijah penetrated the atoms and precipitated an abundance of rain. Jesus used the same dynamic power of thought to break the bonds of the atoms composing the few loaves and fishes of a little lad's lunch—and five thousand persons were fed.

Science is discovering the miracle-working dynamics of religion, but science has not yet comprehended the dynamic directive power of man's thought. All so-called miracle workers claim that they do not of themselves produce the marvelous results; that they are only the instruments of a superior entity.

Jesus said, "He that believeth on me, the works that I do shall he do also." As I go on in the exercise of spiritual faculties I shall strengthen them and understand them better and I shall cease to talk about anything as miraculous.

I affirm: *"The clear unclouded mind of Jesus Christ dominates all my thinking, and I discern the omnipresent laws of Spirit."*

The Overcomer

5th (Passion) Sunday. Read John 20:19-31.

An overcomer is one who recognizes the Truth of his being and is renewing his mind and body and affairs by changing his thoughts from the old mortal beliefs to the new as he sees them in Divine Mind. He is one who demonstrates the divine law, not only in surface life but in innermost consciousness. Spiritual power, mastery, and dominion are attained by the overcomer. "He that overcometh, I will give to him to sit down with me in my throne."

The way of overcoming is, first, to place one's self by faith in the realization of sonship, and secondly, to demonstrate it faithfully in every thought and act. One of the laws of mind is that man becomes like that with which he identifies himself. Christ is the one perfect pattern. Everyone desires to overcome all errors. Each should, therefore, be wise and identify himself with the Christ.

No external condition or circumstance can hold man in bondage when he makes mental contact with God.

It was to the overcomer that Jehovah spoke when, through one of the old prophets, He said, "I will restore to you the years that the locust hath eaten."

We have many blessings. Begin to praise God for the abundance of all things; your words will crack the omnipresent ethers, and good will flow to you from every direction.

The work that I have to do as an overcomer for the world is to help establish a new race consciousness, a new heaven and a new earth, "wherein dwelleth righteousness." By being true to my highest understanding of Truth, I never swerve to the right nor left for any reason.

I affirm: *"I am an overcomer, through Jesus Christ and I rest in the realization of His grace and power."*

Patience

29th Day, Monday. Read Hebrews 11:17-40; 12:1-6.

Patience is a state of mind that beholds the world from the harmony of the Christ Mind, a freedom from personal thinking. It is an attitude of mind characterized by poise, calmness, and a quiet restful trust, especially in the face of trying conditions. It has its foundation in love. "Great peace have they that love thy law; and they have no occasion of stumbling."

The first requisite in the development of patience is spiritual understanding. The larger our vision of life, the more freedom we feel, and we are spared the friction and frettings that come to those who are centered in personality.

Whether one is patient or not depends on his view of life. If he is selfish and self-centered and lives in a material world, bound by his own interests, he lacks the qualities that go to make up patience.

We may take the gift of patience and make use of it. We may receive it by faith, and then work it out in every department of our being by daily practice of Truth.

Patience gives self-control. We unfold the capacity to direct our behavior in right ways, a result of spirituality.

I realize that I am feeding my consciousness on divine patience. When my thoughts are in harmony with divine law, they develop my body into God's beautiful, indestructible temple. "Let us run with patience the race that is set before us, looking unto Jesus the author and perfecter of *our* faith."

I affirm: *"The serene, calm, trustful Spirit now accomplishes all the desires of my heart. I rest in peace."*

Divine Judgment

30th Day, Tuesday. Read Luke 6:37-49.

Human judgment is the mental act of evaluation through comparison or contrast. Intellectual man always judges his fellow man. Divine judgment is of spiritual consciousness. When we awaken to the reality of our divinity, the light begins to break on us from within, and we know the Truth; this is the quickening of our judgment faculty. This faculty may be exercised in two ways: from sense perception or spiritual understanding. If its action be based on sense, its conclusions are fallible and often condemnatory; if on spiritual understanding, they are safe.

The judgment faculty discerns Truth and balances the faculties in righteousness. In the Scriptures judgment is often applied to the action of Divine Mind in its work of judging, especially to the experiences that come to man through the working of the law of justice. Man redeems this faculty by placing it in the Absolute, by declaring and realizing that its origin is in God and all its conclusions are based on Truth. This gives a working center from which the I AM begins to set our thought world in order.

I do not judge others as regards their guilt or innocence. I consider myself and how I stand in the sight of the Father. I begin reform with myself. The judgment seat of Christ is within me, and a judging, or discerning between the true and the false is going on daily in me as an overcomer; I am daily reaping the results of my thoughts and my deed.

I affirm: *"My judgment is just, because I seek not my own will, but the will of the Father."*

Spiritual Substance

31st Day, Wednesday. Read Matthew 13:3-9, 18-23.

There is a kingdom of abundance of all things, and it may be found by those who seek it and are willing to comply with its laws. Substance exists in a realm of ideas and is powerful when handled by one who is familiar with its characteristics.

Spiritual substance is the source of all material wealth and cannot suffer loss or destruction by human thought. It is always with us, ready to be used and to make the consciousness potent and fertile. In this connection Jesus said, "I have meat to eat that ye know not."

Just as the earth is the universal matrix in which all vegetation develops, so this invisible Spirit substance is the universal matrix in which ideas of prosperity germinate and grow and bring forth according to our faith and trust.

I know that any seed words that are planted in omnipresent Spirit substance will germinate and grow and bring forth fruit "after their kind." Just as the farmer selects the best seed for planting, so I must choose the words that will bring forth the rich harvest of plenty.

To gain control of Spirit substance I grasp it with my mind; that is, lay hold of the idea back of it. Right thinking is necessary in using my mind constructively to bring about right results.

I affirm: *"Divine substance flows in all its fullness into my consciousness and through me as prosperity into all my affairs."*

The Atonement

32d Day, Thursday. Read John 17:1-26.

Jesus played a most important part in opening the way for mankind into the Father's kingdom. This was accomplished by His overcoming the belief in death.

Atonement means the reconciliation between God and men through Christ. Jesus became the way by which all who accept Him may "pass over" to the higher consciousness. We have atonement through Him.

"Christ . . . who his own self bare our sins in his body upon the tree, that we, having died unto sins, might live unto righteousness; by whose stripes ye were healed."

The whole race was caught in the meshes of its own thought and, through drowsy ignorance, would have remained there had not a break been made in the structure, and the light of a higher way let in.

If you were held in the meshes of a great spider web, and someone made a hole through which you could pass, you would go where the hole was and would make your escape that way. Jesus made this aperture in the race thought and thus threw open wide the door into the spiritual realm.

His Christianity had a living God in it, a God that lived in Him and spoke through Him. It is a religion of life, as well as purity. Men are to be alive; not merely exist half dead for a few years and then go out with a sputter, like a tallow dip. Christ's men are to be lights that glow with a perpetual current from the one omnipresent energy.

Declaring my unity with this power, I affirm: *"The redeeming word of Jesus Christ, 'I am the resurrection, and the life,' makes me whole and perfect."*

Mount of Transfiguration

33d Day, Friday. Read Matthew 17:1-13.

Transfiguration is always preceded by a change of mind. In transfiguration, ideals are lifted from the material to the spiritual.

Going up into the mountain to pray means an elevation of thought and aspiration from the mortal to the spiritual viewpoint. When the mind is exalted in prayer the rapid radiation of mental energy causes a dazzling light radiation from all parts of the body, and especially the head.

Even our so-called physical body reveals a radiant body, (which Jesus referred to as sitting on the throne of His glory), which interlaces the trillions of cells of the organism and burns brightly. Jesus gave His disciples a glimpse of His radiant body when He was transfigured before them. "His face did shine as the sun, and his garments became white as the light."

He was very advanced in spiritual consciousness and was developed to a larger degree than anyone else in our race. But we all have that body of light, and its development is in proportion to our spiritual culture. Jesus did not go down to corruption but, by the intensity of His spiritual devotions, transformed every cell into its innate divine light and power. When John was in the spirit of devotion Jesus appeared to him and "his eyes were as a flame of fire; and his feet like unto burnished brass." Jesus lives today in that body of glorified light in a kingdom that interpenetrates the earth and its environment.

Jesus is my Way-Shower. In His name I affirm: *"My mind and body are radiant with the light of Spirit, and I am triumphant, glorious, splendid."*

Transmutation

34th Day, Saturday. Read John 2:1-11.

Transmutation—"The conversion of one element into another."—*Webster.*

In consciousness transmutation is a changing in action and character to conform to spiritual standards. It is well said that the mind is the crucible in which the ideal is transmuted into the real.

Jesus said that all power was given to Him in heaven and in earth. He manifested His power in a small way by multiplying a few loaves and fishes to feed more than five thousand persons. In various other instances He demonstrated that He had an understanding of the transmutation of substance. He raised His flesh body to an energy level far higher in potential life and substance than any reached before. We see that not only the mind but also the body is affected in the process of developing out of the natural into the spiritual.

The leaven of the Pharisees and of Herod (Mark 8:15) represents limited thoughts. When we attempt to confine the divine law to the customary avenues of expression and scoff at anything beyond, we are letting the leaven of the Pharisees work in us. When the mind is raised up through affirmation to God's omnipresent substance and life, we are not only fed, but there is a surplus. This is the teaching of Jesus, and it has always been exemplified by His faithful followers.

I realize that through the law of transmutation every error thought in my consciousness is transmuted into its spiritual correspondence.

I affirm: *"Spirit in me is transmuting my body into pure spiritual substance, and my soul rejoices."*

Palm Sunday

Palm Sunday. Read John 12:12-50.

Palm Sunday is the Sunday preceding Easter.

Jerusalem, the Holy City, symbolizes within us the habitation of peace, possession of peace, vision of peace, abode of prosperity within us.

In man Jerusalem is the abiding consciousness of spiritual peace, which is the result of continuous realizations of spiritual power tempered with spiritual poise and confidence. Jerusalem symbolizes the great nerve center just back of the heart. From this point Spirit sends its radiance to all parts of the body.

Jesus symbolizes our I AM identity. His going up to Jerusalem means our taking the last step in unfoldment preparatory to the final step, when the personality is entirely crucified and the Christ triumphs.

Jesus riding the ass into Jerusalem means the fulfillment of the time when the spiritual I AM within us takes control and lifts all the animal forces up to the spiritual plane of mastery, purity, and peace.

When the I AM takes charge of the body a new order of things is inaugurated. The vitality is no longer wasted. Through high and pure ideals the whole consciousness is raised to a higher standard.

The hosannas of the rejoicing multitude and the spreading of their garments and branches of trees before Jesus, represent joyful obedience and homage that all the thoughts in one's consciousness give when an error state of mind is overcome. "Blessed *is* he that cometh in the name of the Lord."

In the name of Jesus Christ I affirm: *"The Spirit of Him that raised up Jesus dwells in me, and I am made perfect."*

The New Race

35th Day, Monday. Read Revelation 21:1-7; 22: 1-7.

"These things shall be! a loftier race
Than e'er the world hath known shall rise

With flame of freedom in their souls,
And light of knowledge in their eyes.

* * *

"Nation with nation, land with land,
Unarmed shall live as comrades free:
In every heart and brain shall throb
The pulse of one fraternity."

The time is ripe for the advent of a new race, the advent of the spiritualized man. This will be brought about, not by a miracle or the fiat of God, but by the gradual refinement of the man of the flesh into the man of Spirit.

The true overcomer is qualifying himself to become a member of this superrace. It is well for such a one to cultivate the childlike spirit and let go of all tense striving, even for spiritual things. In the realization of protecting, providing love, all the strain of fear and anxiety will be removed and life in abundance will then find easy entrance into the consciousness, bringing strength and health and eternal youth and life.

Spiritual harmony in man depends largely on the right relation of the inner and the outer realms of his consciousness. Expression is the law of life. Whatever is expressed becomes manifest. I realize that as an overcomer, I am working also for the whole world, establishing a new race consciousness, "new heavens and a new earth."

I affirm: *"The redeeming law of God is awakening with me, and I am a new man in Christ Jesus."*

The Fire of God

36th Day, Tuesday. Read Acts 2:1-21.

Fire represents the positive, affirmative state of mind, as opposed to the negative or watery state.

The fire of God (Holy Spirit) is the Word of God in action. It burns out the dross of negation in consciousness, and reveals Christ. Tongues of fire represent the illumination of thought, in demonstration of Spirit's presence and power. The flame of fire symbolizes the light of intuition that burns in our heart.

While the light of intuition (flame of fire) burns in our heart, there is no loss of substance. In thinking there is a vibratory process that uses up nerve tissue, but in the wisdom that comes from the heart this "bush" or tissue is not consumed. This is "holy ground," or substance in Divine Mind. When man approaches this he must take off from his understanding all limited thoughts of the Absolute ("put off thy shoes from off thy feet").

Spiritual fire is a symbol of the destruction of evil and error. The fire of Spirit never ceases its life-giving, purifying glow. In it all error is burned up in consciousness and the purified man then manifests this "fire" as eternal life.

I have the assurance that I shall not be left partially cleansed, that the purifying work will be complete. "Our God is a consuming fire," also He is life, love, substance, power, intelligence, Truth.

In the name of Jesus Christ, I affirm: "*The Holy Spirit flares its cleansing, purifying flames throughout soul and body, and I am made whole and perfect.*"

Holy Communion

37th Day, Wednesday. Read Luke 22:1-23.

"And as they were eating, Jesus took bread, and blessed, and brake it; and he gave to the disciples, and said, Take, eat; this is my body, And he took a cup, and gave thanks, and gave to them, saying, Drink ye all of it; for this is my blood of the covenant."

The first step in drinking of the blood and eating of the body of Jesus is to resolve this whole Scripture back into the primal ideas. The only way to appropriate these ideas is through the very highest activity of mind as in prayer.

The benefit of taking Holy Communion is the establishing of our acceptance of the Christ whose coming we celebrate within our mind and heart. The bread used in the churches symbolizes substance, which we consider the Lord's body, a body of spiritual ideas; and the wine used symbolizes His blood, which we consider life, or the circulation of divine ideas in our consciousness that will purify our mind and heart and renew our strength, freeing us from all corruption, sin, and evil, and bringing forth in us the abundant, unlimited life of God. Through the appropriation and assimilation of the substance and life in our own consciousness, we blend our minds with the Father-Mind and there is a harmonizing of every fiber of our body with the Christ body, which is life and light. As our mind and heart are cleansed of untrue thoughts and beliefs, and as we feed on living ideas, our body takes on the life and light of our divinity, and eventually will become living light.

I affirm: *"God's pure life and substance are constantly renewing and rebuilding His holy temple, my body."*

Gethsemane

38th Day, Thursday. Read Mark 14:32-42.

Gethsemane is symbolic of the struggle that takes place within the consciousness when Truth is realized as the one reality. It is a condition that man works through when he recognizes that God is all and that he must be willing to sacrifice all for God.

There are always deeply rooted error thoughts stored away in the subconsciousness, and on their own account they come forward to crucify the new unknown power, the so-called imposter, the indwelling Christ. The Christ is presumably captured by these thoughts, which try to carry out their aims in the darkness of the subconscious mind. But error can kill out only error. The Christ itself may be held in obscurity for a while, but it cannot be done away with. That which died on the Cross when Jesus was crucified was the personality; the Christ resurrects itself from the very depths of the subconsciousness, and error is hanged on the gallows it prepared for the doing away of the newborn spiritual ego.

This breaking up and passing away of old error states of mind and making ready for the new is a process in soul evolution of all those who are faithfully following Jesus. In all systems of thought concentration and spiritual attainment, the will, the executive faculty, plays the leading part. Therefore I prepare my consciousness for the reception of these new ideas. I say with Jesus, "Not my will, but thine, be done." I realize that new inspiration is flowing steadily into my consciousness as I affirm: *"Old error thoughts are passed away. I am a new creature in Christ."*

Crucifixion

39th Day, Good Friday. Read John 19:1-42.

Jesus' crucifixion on Calvary was a final step in a work that had been going on in Him for thirty-three years, and when He arose He was entirely free from the carnal mind with all its limitations. He had overcome all the carnal tendencies which He had taken on that He might free the race from its bondage.

The word *crucifixion* means the crossing out in consciousness of certain errors that have become fixed states of mind; it is the enactment by a master of the final extinction of carnal mind, the giving up of the whole personality in order that the Christ Mind may be expressed in all its fullness. This is represented by the crucifixion of Jesus.

Calvary means "the place of a skull." The carnal mind has appropriated the brain and its skull and it is here that the final battle is fought. Every time we give up error there is a crucifixion.

The three days Jesus was in the tomb represent the three steps in overcoming error. First, nonresistance; second, the taking on of divine activity, or receiving the will of God; third, the assimilation and fulfillment of the divine will.

I deny the self that I may unite with the selfless. I give up the mortal that I may attain the immortal. I dissolve the thought of the physical body that I may realize the spiritual body. This is a mental process with a physical effect.

I affirm: *"Yea, though I walk through the valley of the shadow of death, I will fear no evil; for thou art with me; thy rod and thy staff, they comfort me."*

Resting in God

40th Day, Saturday. Read Isaiah 11:1-10; 12:1-6.

After Jesus' crucifixion He was laid to rest in the tomb of Joseph of Arimathea. Jesus represents the expression of the I AM identity. Arimathea represents an aggregation of thoughts of lofty character, a high state of consciousness in man. Joseph represents a state of consciousness in which we improve in character along all lines. We not only grow into a broader understanding but also we increase in vitality and substance. We are resting in God, and at the same time gathering strength for the power of greater demonstrations to follow.

A degree of cleansing, a wiping out of sense consciousness has been accomplished. By mentally reviewing our experiences, we recognize that nothing is really destroyed, but rather transmuted. Through faith we take stock of the progress we have made and find that we are getting a consciousness of radiant substance and of a higher life. Nothing is lost. When sense consciousness is raised to a higher plane all that belongs to it is saved with it.

In reality the invisible cannot be seen, touched, or comprehended by the outer senses, yet in this realm a great and mighty work is being accomplished.

Today I realize that the leaven that "leaveneth the whole lump" is the Truth. The word of Truth within me is not idle, but quietly spreading from point to point. This process will continue until my whole consciousness is vitalized by the Holy Spirit.

I affirm: *"I rest in the consciousness of eternal life and strength, and I am made perfect."*

The Resurrection

Easter Sunday. Read John 20:1-18.

Easter is the celebration of the resurrection of Jesus. Its inner meaning and spiritual significance is the awakening and raising to spiritual consciousness of the I AM in man, which has been dead in trespass and sin and buried in the tomb of materiality.

"I came that they may have life, and may have *it* abundantly." The resurrection is the raising up of the whole man—spirit, soul, and body—into the Christ consciousness of life and wholeness. This Jesus did. The tomb could not hold His redeemed perfected body temple. Resurrection is accomplished by the quickening power of the Holy Spirit.

Every time we rise to the realization of eternal, indwelling life, making union with the Father-Mind, the resurrection of Jesus takes place within us. All thoughts of limitation and inevitable obedience to material law are left in the tomb of materiality.

Jesus was born into the race thought so that He might reconstruct it in conformity with the divine law. He thus became our Way-Shower, our Saviour, our Helper.

Today the light of Truth is illumining my mind, and I rise up in the majesty of my divine sonship and proclaim myself to be the child of the Most High, free from all belief in sin, sickness, and death.

I affirm: *"In unity with Christ I realize that I am resurrected into the life, light, and power of God."*

INDEX

The Unity Lenten Guide

OBSERVE LENT THE UNITY WAY

Unity believes that we can keep Lent best by denying ourselves not "things" but negative thoughts and feelings. And, through prayer and study, we can contemplate the victorious Christ and attempt to be more like Him.

Keep a True Lent contains material especially written by Charles Fillmore to help you observe Lent in this way.

How to Study

1. Before beginning your day-by-day study, we suggest you read all the chapters preceding the Lenten lessons.

2. Set aside a definite time for prayer and study when you are least likely to be interrupted.

3. Read each day's assignment, beginning with Ash Wednesday.

4. Read the Bible reference given at the beginning of each day's lesson.

5. Answer the questions concerning what you have read.

6. Use the meditation given in the Study Guide.

7. Put the principles of these lessons to work in your life.

1st Day **Ash Wednesday**

Reading Assignment: "Denial," page 141; Chapter 9, pages 63-70

Questions:

1. What is denial?
2. What should follow denial?
3. How should denials be made?
4. How are quarrels and uncharitable thoughts overcome?

I keep a true Lent by denying limiting beliefs of the past and by laying hold of positive ideas that are life-giving. Thus I spiritualize my thinking and transform my life.

2d Day **Affirmation**

Reading Assignment: "Affirmation," page 142; Chapter 10, pages 71-76

Questions:

1. What is an affirmation?
2. What is the result of many affirmations?
3. What is the highest affirmation we can make?
4. What happens when one lives affirmations of Truth?

In time of need I will remind myself and declare: "I am God's child, created in His image and likeness. I am joint heir with Jesus Christ to the kingdom of God."

God **3d Day**

Reading Assignment: "God," page 143; Chapter 2, pages 14, 15; Chapter 4, pages 24, 25

Questions:

1. How are God's attributes brought into expression?
2. Why was Jesus a true expression of God? Explain.
3. What must we do to make ourselves channels through which God can come forth into expression?
4. What is our inheritance from God?

Jesus thought, spoke, and acted in accord with His divine Self. I too think, speak, and act in accord with my divine Self.

I AM **4th Day**

Reading Assignment: "I AM," page 144; Chapter 2, pages 14-18; Chapter 3, pages 20, 21; Chapter 8, page 56; Chapter 15, page 121

Questions:

1. Explain the I AM.
2. Where is the home of I AM?
3. What is the rock foundation of being?
4. What happens when we build our consciousness in God-Mind?

I am free to live healthily and happily. I am free to express my talents and abilities. I am free to go forward in peace and joy.

1st Sunday **The Altar**

Reading Assignment: "The Altar," page 145; Chapter 11, page 83; Chapter 13, page 95

Questions:

1. What does going to the altar signify?
2. What is the altar to the unknown God?
3. What happens when we pray?
4. What part does desire play in our spiritual growth?

Let me remember always that prayer does not change God—prayer changes me. Prayer brings me closer to God, closer to the light, closer to Truth.

5th Day **The Garden of Eden**

Reading Assignment: "The Garden of Eden," page 147; Chapter 17, pages 130-135

Questions:

1. What is man's primary work in the earthly consciousness?
2. What is the Garden?
3. Explain the importance of the power of thought.
4. What do the twelve gates that open into the Garden of Eden represent?

Lent is a splendid time to build a strong consciousness of life. I affirm again and again that my body is the temple of the living God.

Faith **6th Day**

Reading Assignment: "Faith," page 148; Chapter 15, pages 110-121

Questions:

1. Define "faith."
2. How is the faith center developed?
3. Where should we place our faith?
4. What happens when the mental eye is illumined with faith?

Faith is one of my inborn faculties; I need only begin to use it. As I keep it turned in the direction of Truth, my faith grows and develops.

Strength **7th Day**

Reading Assignment: "Strength," page 149; Chapter 3, pages 19-23

Questions:

1. Define "strength."
2. Where does strength originate?
3. How can we establish strength in soul and body?
4. Why is strength of spirit necessary?

I am strong in the Lord and in the power of His might. As I turn to Him in prayer, my mind is open to ideas that are strong and true, and I feel an inflow of strength.

8th Day **Wisdom**

Reading Assignment: "Wisdom," page 150; Chapter 8, pages 56, 57

Questions:

1. Where does wisdom originate?
2. What is the difference between wisdom and understanding?
3. How do we become conscious of the Christ radiance?
4. What does spiritual understanding reveal?

The Christ light, the light of Truth, is shining at the heart of my being. My thoughts are illumined by the light of Spirit and my powers and capabilities are increased.

9th Day **Love**

Reading Assignment: "Love," page 151; Chapter 5, pages 30-35

Questions:

1. Define "love."
2. What happens when love is made active in consciousness?
3. What is necessary to make a perfect union between our mind and the loving mind of the Father?
4. Is there any bar to our exercise of love?

I express love to all, love that is balanced with wisdom. My prayer is: "Lord, make me a channel for the expression of Your love, day by day."

Power 10th Day

Reading Assignment: "Power," page 153; Chapter 10, pages 73, 74; Chapter 15, pages 113-121

Questions:

1. What must precede man's control of his thoughts and feelings?
2. What is the highest gift given to man?
3. How does the voice become rich, warm, and mellow?
4. What happens when we pray and realize our spiritual dominion?

The Truth is that I can do all things through the power of Christ working within me. I can act and react in loving ways. I can find harmony and happiness in living with the people in my world.

Imagination 2d Sunday

Reading Assignment: "Imagination," page 154; Chapter 7, page 52

Questions:

1. Define "imagination."
2. How was everything that exists brought into expression?
3. How do we lay hold of ideas?
4. What part does the imagining power of the mind play in our communication with God?

I allow my mind to run to positive imagery. I see my life as it is meant to be—good and beautiful.

11th Day **Understanding**

Reading Assignment: "Understanding," page 155; Chapter 7, pages 45, 46; Chapter 17, pages 127, 128

Questions:

1. Define "spiritual understanding."
2. What does understanding reveal?
3. What is it in us that comprehends?
4. Why must we develop understanding?

I open my mind to light and understanding. I give thanks that the glory and the brightness of Christ shine in me and through me.

12th Day **Will**

Reading Assignment: "Will," page 156; Chapter 8, pages 61, 62; Chapter 15, page 110

Questions:

1. Define "will."
2. What teaches us the Father's will?
3. How does man form spiritual character?
4. How do we bring the divine will to bear in our consciousness?

If I have hesitated to pray, "Not my will, but thine, be done," I now know that the will of God is good, and I will to do God's will.

Law 13th Day

Reading Assignment: "Law," page 158; Chapter 5, page 32; Chapter 17, page 131

Questions:

1. What is divine law?
2. What is divine law in us?
3. Does man make the law? Explain.
4. How does man align himself with divine law?

Father-God, give me the wisdom and understanding to see Your divine law of good at work in every part of my life. Let me walk unafraid through every experience, secure in the knowledge that You are always present.

Zeal 14th Day

Reading Assignment: "Zeal," page 159; Chapter 10, pages 71-76

Questions:

1. Define "zeal."
2. What part does zeal play in achievement?
3. Can zeal become excessive? Explain.
4. For what purpose should a portion of zeal be used?

Father-God, I pray for zeal to motivate me to achievement, and for wisdom to keep me steady, strong, and true to divine principle.

15th Day **Renunciation**

Reading Assignment: "Renunciation," page 160; Chapter 9, pages 63-70

Questions:

1. For what purpose did Jesus come?
2. How did Jesus convey to us the truth that there is no power and no reality in sin?
3. What happens when we enter into an understanding of the real?
4. What in us discerns the difference between Truth and error?

I rejoice in the truth that there is no power and no reality in sin. The place in my thoughts that had been occupied with past disappointment and past mistakes is now filled with an understanding of God's freeing love.

16th Day **Life**

Reading Assignment: "Life," page 161; Chapter 8, pages 60, 61; Chapter 16, pages 122-126

Questions:

1. How does life manifest itself?
2. Where does life originate?
3. What was the God presence to Jesus?
4. How do we make alive all the cells of our organism?

Christ within me is my life. Every part of my body temple is filled with the vigor and strength of Christ.

Conservation **3d Sunday**

Reading Assignment: "Conservation," page 162; Chapter 9, pages 69, 70

Questions:

1. What happens to our youth?
2. How can we regain our youth?
3. What does Jesus represent?
4. What step is necessary in the process of body restoration?

I live with the realization that the Christ in me is eternally renewing every cell and atom of my entire being.

Jesus Christ Our Helper **17th Day**

Reading Assignment: "Jesus Christ Our Helper," page 164; Chapter 2, page 17

Questions:

1. What reason have we for believing that God planned to make Jesus a continuous working factor in our civilization?
2. What did Jesus promise?
3. How did Jesus become a citizen of heaven?
4. Why do we not see Jesus?

I have an important assignment: It is to follow the Jesus Christ way as closely as I am able, so that I too may bless, inspire, and uplift others.

18th Day **Evolution**

Reading Assignment: "Evolution," page 165; Chapter 4, page 27

Questions:

1. What is enfolded in every man?
2. Define "evolution."
3. What is the supreme attainment of every man?
4. How did God project man and the universe into creation?

Spiritual growth cannot be forced. It is an upward journey, and each time I pray, each time I affirm Truth, I am adding to my spiritual consciousness.

19th Day **The Blood of Jesus**

Reading Assignment: "The Blood of Jesus," page 166; Chapter 4, page 28; Chapter 17, page 134

Questions:

1. How did Jesus purify the natural blood in His body?
2. How did Jesus broadcast the spiritual electrons of His body into the race thought atmosphere?
3. How do we partake of the substance and life of Spirit and build the Christ body?
4. Where does the way to eternal life lie?

As I let my mind dwell on the nature of Jesus Christ, I absorb more of His Spirit into my consciousness. His strength becomes my strength. His life becomes my life. His power becomes my power.

The Body Temple — 20th Day

Reading Assignment: "The Body Temple," page 167; Chapter 3, pages 19-23

Questions:

1. How can we have a perfect body and a perfect world?
2. How does the mind lay hold of Truth?
3. What does it mean to bless someone or something?
4. What is the result of our spiritual thought?

I keep my attention on the ageless, perfect Spirit within me.

The Grace of God — 21st Day

Reading Assignment: "The Grace of God," page 168; Chapter 4, pages 24, 25

Questions:

1. Define "grace."
2. How far does the grace of God extend?
3. How may we become recipients of that which the Father would bestow?
4. How does the redeeming, transforming power come to us?

Through the grace of God I forgive, and I am forgiven.

22d Day — Fourth Dimension

Reading Assignment: "Fourth Dimension," page 170; Chapter 15, page 110

Questions:

1. Define the "fourth dimension."
2. What binds the human mind?
3. What happens when we invoke the aid of Christ?
4. How do we enter the realm of the fourth dimension?

Through Christ within, I clearly discern spiritual things. I know that there is no limit to the width of my human horizon when I realize my divine potential.

4th Sunday — The Sabbath

Reading Assignment: "The Sabbath," page 171; Chapter 11, pages 77-86

Questions:

1. What is the true Sabbath?
2. What does the seventh day mean?
3. How is man raised out of the Adam consciousness?
4. Does God rest? Explain.

I daily emphasize the Sabbath idea, the idea of serving God in praise and thanksgiving, and in silent prayer.

The Idea **23d Day**

Reading Assignment: "The Idea," page 172; Chapter 7, pages 48, 49; Chapter 15, page 119

Questions:

1. Define "idea."
2. What happens when ideas are released?
3. How do we bring divine ideas into manifestation?
4. How did Jesus heal the sick and raise the dead?

I am in touch with God's infinite storehouse of divine ideas. I use these divine ideas in my daily living.

Healing **24th Day**

Reading Assignment: "Healing," page 173; Chapter 3, pages 19-23

Questions:

1. What is the normal condition of man?
2. What is the first step in spiritual healing? The next?
3. How did the early Christians do their mighty works?
4. How do we raise our consciousness to spirituality?

Quietly, confidently, I turn to God. His vitalizing life and energy floods my whole being. I am healed. Praise God, I am healed.

25th Day **Peace**

Reading Assignment: "Peace," page 175; Chapter 1, pages 9-13

Questions:

1. What releases spiritual ideas of far-reaching influence?
2. How did Jesus handle antagonism?
3. What did Jesus know in regard to the universal law of justice?
4. How is justice established in our affairs?

My mind is stayed on Thee, O Lord. I place myself and all that concerns me trustingly in Thy care. I rest in Thy peace and power.

26th Day **Heaven**

Reading Assignment: "Heaven," page 176; Chapter 14, pages 107, 108

Questions:

1. What are the two universal planes of consciousness?
2. How do they differ?
3. How does God create?
4. Where is heaven?

I do not look to a future time nor to a distant place for heaven. Here and now I am at one with the kingdom of all good.

Principle — 27th Day

Reading Assignment: "Principle," page 177; Chapter 2, page 14; Chapter 9, page 69

Questions:

1. Define "principle."
2. How can we demonstrate principle?
3. What unifies us with Divine Mind?
4. How may we realize the perfect mind which was in Christ Jesus?

I apply divine principles to my problems when I seek spiritual help, when I turn to God with my needs. As I pray, God reveals right answers; He fulfills my every need.

Miracles — 28th Day

Reading Assignment: "Miracles," page 178; Chapter 10, page 75

Questions:

1. Explain the first miracle in our consciousness.
2. What are miracles?
3. Does God perform miracles? Explain.
4. What do miracle workers claim?

I may consider the works of Jesus as miraculous, but He considered them the outcome of the operation of divine law. I, too, can use the dynamic power of right thinking and prayer to bring healing where healing is needed and blessings where blessings are needed.

5th Sunday **The Overcomer**

Reading Assignment: "The Overcomer," page 180; Chapter 6, page 38

Questions:

1. Define an "overcomer."
2. How does one become an overcomer?
3. What is one of the laws of mind?
4. What is the work we have to do as overcomers?

I claim my dominion in Christ. I affirm my freedom to express the Christ perfection within me.

29th Day **Patience**

Reading Assignment: "Patience," page 181; Chapter 5, pages 30-35

Questions:

1. Define "patience."
2. What is the first requisite in developing patience?
3. What happens if we are self-centered and live in a material world?
4. What does patience give us?

I am patient, for my faith in God assures me that all things in my life are working together for my good.

Divine Judgment — 30th Day

Reading Assignment: "Divine Judgment," page 182; Chapter 12, pages 87-92

Questions:

1. What is human judgment?
2. What is divine judgment?
3. How is our judgment faculty quickened?
4. How do we redeem our judgment faculty?

As I cease to misjudge other persons, I find that I am not misjudged. I find that there is no criticism or condemnation in me, for me, or against me.

Spiritual Substance — 31st Day

Reading Assignment: "Spiritual Substance," page 183; Chapter 1, page 11; Chapter 2, page 14

Questions:

1. How may the kingdom of abundance be found?
2. Where does substance exist?
3. What is spiritual substance?
4. How can we gain control of Spirit substance?

If I have a need of any kind, I open myself to the substance of Spirit. I give thanks that there is abundant supply for every need.

32d Day — The Atonement

Reading Assignment: "The Atonement," page 185; Chapter 7, page 53

Questions:

1. How did Jesus open the way for mankind into the Father's kingdom?
2. What does "atonement" mean?
3. What would have happened to mankind if Jesus had not come?
4. Describe the Christianity of Jesus.

I am one with God, He is one with me. God is in me as the light that shines, dissipating all darkness, radiating into every part of my life.

33d Day — Mount of Transfiguration

Reading Assignment: "Mount of Transfiguration," page 186; Chapter 16, pages 125, 126

Questions:

1. What precedes transfiguration?
2. What happens when the mind is exalted in prayer?
3. Do we all have a body of light? Explain.
4. How did Jesus transform His body?

Jesus referred to us as children of light. I am a child of light. I have a mind filled with light, a body filled with light. I am shining, glorious, splendid.

Transmutation **34th Day**

Reading Assignment: "Transmutation," page 187; Chapter 10, page 75

Questions:

1. Define "transmutation."
2. What is transmutation in consciousness?
3. What is affected in the process of developing out of the natural into the spiritual?
4. What does it mean to let the leaven of the Pharisees work in us?

There is no condition of mind or body that cannot be lifted up. Spirit in me, God's spirit, is powerful and ever-present. Spirit is life-giving.

Palm Sunday

Reading Assignment: "Palm Sunday," page 188; Chapter 5, page 34

Questions:

1. What does Jerusalem symbolize?
2. What does Jesus symbolize?
3. What does Jesus' going to Jerusalem symbolize?
4. What happens when I AM takes charge?

The transcending spirit of Christ is in me. Abiding in this realization, I am at peace. I am poised and confident.

35th Day **The New Race**

Reading Assignment: "The New Race," page 189; Chapter 8, pages 54-62

Questions:

1. How will the advent of a new race be brought about?
2. Who will qualify to be a member of this new race?
3. What should the true overcomer do?
4. Upon what does spiritual harmony in man depend?

I never cease to grow and progress. Each day I am inspired through Christ in me to come up higher and nearer to His perfection.

36th Day **The Fire of God**

Reading Assignment: "The Fire of God," page 191; Chapter 9, page 68

Questions:

1. What does fire represent?
2. What is the fire of God?
3. What does the fire of God do?
4. What must we do when we approach holy ground?

The works of Spirit are always constructive. I am not afraid to be on fire with the idea of God; I am not afraid to be consumed with a desire for greater light and Truth.

Holy Communion — 37th Day

Reading Assignment: "Holy Communion," page 192; Chapter 17, pages 113, 134

Questions:

1. What is the first step in drinking of the blood and eating of the body of Jesus?
2. What is the benefit of taking Holy Communion?
3. What does bread symbolize?
4. What does wine symbolize?

I observe Holy Communion by keeping the words of Jesus Christ before me, by letting His words of Truth grow in my mind, and by following in His footsteps.

Gethsemane — 38th Day

Reading Assignment: "Gethsemane," page 193; Chapter 9, page 64

Questions:

1. What does Gethsemane symbolize?
2. What is the function of error thoughts in the subconscious?
3. What was crucified on the Cross?
4. What plays the leading part in spiritual attainment?

I call on God's power to dissolve old error thoughts. I let my thoughts follow after the pattern of Truth set for me by Jesus Christ.

39th Day **Good Friday** **Crucifixion**

Reading Assignment: "Crucifixion," page 194; Chapter 17, pages 133, 134

Questions:

1. What was the final step of Jesus' work?
2. What does the word "crucifixion" mean?
3. What does "calvary" mean?
4. What do the three days Jesus was in the tomb represent?

God's spirit in me is invincible and indestructible. Thank You, Father, for Your spirit in me that gives me victory over death itself.

40th Day **Resting in God**

Reading Assignment: "Resting in God," page 195; Chapter 5, page 30

Questions:

1. What does Arimathea represent?
2. What does Joseph represent?
3. What happens when sense consciousness is raised to a higher plane?
4. What is the leaven that "leaveneth the whole lump"?

Father-God, I rest in the consciousness of Your presence within me and about me. I rest in the consciousness of Your life and perfection within me.

The Resurrection **Easter Sunday**

Reading Assignment: "The Resurrection," page 197; Chapter 1, page 13; Chapter 3, page 21

Questions:

1. What is the spiritual significance of Easter?
2. What is the resurrection?
3. How is resurrection accomplished?
4. Why was Jesus born into the race thought?

Christ within me is the resurrection and the life. Christ within me is the power that enables me to rise triumphant out of every trial.

About the Author

Charles Fillmore was an innovative thinker, a pioneer in metaphysical thought at a time when most religious thought in America was entirely orthodox. He was a lifelong advocate of the open, inquiring mind, and he took pride in keeping abreast of the latest scientific and educational discoveries and theories. Many years ago he wrote, "What you think today may not be the measure for your thought tomorrow"; and it seems likely that were he to compile this book today, he might use different metaphors, different scientific references, and so on.

Truth is changeless. Those who knew Charles Fillmore best believe that he would like to be able to rephrase some of his observations for today's readers, thus giving them the added effectiveness of contemporary thought. But the ideas themselves—the core of Charles Fillmore's writings—are as timeless now (and will be tomorrow) as when they were first published.

Charles Fillmore was born on an Indian reservation just outside the town of St. Cloud, Minnesota, on August 22, 1854. He made his transition on July 5, 1948, at Unity Village, Missouri, at the age of 93. To get a sense of history, when Charles was eleven, Abraham Lincoln was assassinated; when Charles died, Harry Truman was President.

With his wife Myrtle, Charles Fillmore founded the Unity movement and Silent Unity, the international prayer ministry that publishes *Daily Word.* Charles and Myrtle built the worldwide organization that continues their work today, Unity School of Christianity. Through

Unity School's ministries of prayer, education, and publishing, millions of people around the world are finding the teachings of Truth discovered and practiced by Charles and Myrtle Fillmore.

Charles Fillmore was a spiritual pioneer whose impact has yet to be assessed. No lesser leaders than Dr. Norman Vincent Peale and Dr. Emmet Fox were profoundly influenced by him. Dr. Peale borrowed his catchphrase of *positive thinking* from Charles Fillmore. Emmet Fox was so affected by Fillmore's ideas that he changed his profession. From an engineer, he became the well-known writer and speaker.

Charles Fillmore—author, teacher, metaphysician, practical mystic, husband, father, spiritual leader, visionary—has left a legacy that continues to impact the lives of millions of people. By his fruits, he is continuously known.

Printed in the U.S.A. 96-1245-10M-6-99